THE SOCIALIZATION OF THE AFRICAN AMERICAN CHILD:

In Contemporary America

SEKOU CLINCY

authorHOUSE®

AuthorHouse™
1663 Liberty Drive
Bloomington, IN 47403
www.authorhouse.com
Phone: 1-800-839-8640

First published by AuthorHouse 2/15/2011

ISBN: 978-1-4490-8787-6 (sc)
ISBN: 978-1-4490-8788-3 (dj)
ISBN: 978-1-4490-8789-0 (e)

Printed in the United States of America

Any people depicted in stock imagery provided by Thinkstock are models, and such images are being used for illustrative purposes only. Certain stock imagery © Thinkstock.

This book is printed on acid-free paper.

DEDICATIONS

This book is dedicated to Dr. Harold Aldridge Jr. and future generations of children and youth. It is my hope that you search for truth and make this world a better place.

ACKNOWLEDGEMENT – THANK YOU

THIS BOOK WOULD NOT HAVE been written without the encouragement, commitment, and help of a talented group of people. First, my thanks go to the countless parents and caregivers, and extended kinship who share a genuine concern for African American children and culture. Thanks also to all of the researchers who provided invaluable insight and scientific information in the beginning stages of this book. A warm thank you to all of the children and staff I've worked with over the years as a counselor, recruiter, fatherhood coordinator, and health education specialist. Extra special thanks to the University of Oklahoma for all of its resources. Thank you to the Clincy, Grimmett, and Collins' families for their time, advice, and support. Thank you, Gwen and Lisa for all of your brilliance. I couldn't have made it without you two.

Thanks to all of the scholars and people in the trenches who sacrificed time and family to give birth to this book.

FOREWORD

—▶ ◀—

THE WORK OF MR. CLINCY is very timely and very important to the current state of African American children across the United States. In unprecedented numbers, there is senseless teen violence, teen pregnancy starting at the ages of 12 & 13, and the ages of youthful offenders starting earlier than has been seen in any recent time. The one place that should serve as a safe haven and sanctuary (the schools) is failing the urban and underprivileged student. These are situations in which African Americans live daily. How can we expect these children to rise above this reality if they are not shown an alternative?

In reading *The Socialization of the African American Child,* I had to pause and perform a self-assessment/self-reflection to determine how I was not one of the children discussed in this work. From 0 to 9 years of age, I grew up in an urban neighborhood. Our neighbors were a mix of retired Black senior citizens; grandmothers raising their children and grandchildren; two parent homes; and single parent homes. The stereotypes typically displayed in the media were present. The reality was not as exaggerated as the media depictions. I vividly recall my parents letting my brothers and I know that although we lived in this environment we were not part of this environment. My parents had high expectations of us because they wanted more and better opportunities for us than they had.

To ensure that their children were successful, both of my parents were present and active in our lives. We were taught right from wrong. My parents were involved in homework and encouraged extra-curricular activities of our interest. There were no limits placed on our dreams. The one constant was that education was the key to whatever we decided to do.

I was fortunate in my educational experiences. My experiences in both the urban and what is called the 'mainstream' school districts were of teachers pushing their students to excel. Students identified as 'gifted' were either given extra credit work or placed in classes that exposed the students to different subjects. For example, I was enrolled in a mythology class in the 5th grade, and in the 8th grade I was selected to take Algebra I. (In the 80s it was uncommon for Algebra to be taken so early.) There was also more of a focus of students mentoring fellow students. In the schools I attended, there were tutoring classes where students who were struggling could go to get help. Lastly, teachers were more focused on preparing students for college than teaching to pass standardized tests.

What we are now seeing is more students failing at earlier ages because the pace of instruction has quickened to ensure all material of the standardized test is covered. The basics of what I am familiar with is not being taught at a sufficient level. The unintended effect is a low level of retention of the material that is being taught to students. This is particularly troubling for African American and disadvantaged students who are in urban neighborhoods.

To this end, I am part of a non-profit organization, Making Better C.H.O.I.C.E.S., whose vision is to serve disadvantaged communities and to aid and empower disenfranchised individuals both socially and economically. We want to help the disadvantaged develop the necessary tools and skills to be assets in their communities. The African American community is our particular interest.

Our work focuses on developing programs to address the educational, the economic, and the social needs of the African American community. Our biggest challenge will be to understand the environment in which these children are exposed to and develop programs that are relevant to their world. African American children are exposed to so much more than what I was exposed to at their age. Children now are influenced by their peers, media (entertainment), and in some instances familial relations. These influences in most instances are negative and do not provide these children with a sense of hope or an opportunity for an alternative. This is where *The Socialization of the African American Child* is such an asset to Making Better C.H.O.I.C.E.S., Inc. Our vision of empowering African American children cannot happen without first understanding where we came from and why we are where we are. The material in this book is an essential piece to that understanding.

Lisa A. White – Sagacity Management Consultants, LLC

TABLE OF CONTENTS

LIST OF TABLES AND FIGURES

— → —

THE AUTHOR CAN BE CONTACTED AT S_CLINCY@HOTMAIL.COM

INTRODUCTION

THE CHIEF AIM OF THIS book is to afford readers a comprehensive view of the current state of the African American experience and how it shapes the child/youth's perspective. Oftentimes, members within and outside the community fail to objectively critique this culture. Not understanding African American history and how it relates to the socialization process perpetuates the worst of this culture, rather than the best.

Today, we have occurrences that are unprecedented in the history of America: a vast divide between the rich and poor, irreversible environmental damage, over half of African American children living in single-parent households, and high incarceration rates among African American young people. When oppressed folk are driven into desperate channels, criminal activity is likely to follow. Thus it is imperative to take a good look at what black people are doing and not doing as parents or immediate caregivers, which ultimately will determine the future of the black race. It is equally imperative to study the past. Indeed, when a people don't know who they are—their history—they perish. This fact should motivate us to move in unparalleled directions toward survival.

Too much time and effort is invested mimicking what is viewed on television as opposed to practicing love, moral vision, and leadership. These elements are often afforded by grandparents, if they're in the youth's life. The emotional bonds grandparents provide their grandchildren are noted in the Kornhaber and Woodward (1981) study (see Ann C. Taylor).

Throughout my years of counseling, countless impoverished parents expressed their interest in sending their children to a private or better public school. The greatest hindrance was lack of finances. In the educational sector of this work, I examine other obstacles that poor schoolchildren—

namely, African American—grapple with in public schools. Most African American children are bright and eager to learn educational material that relates to them. The struggle is that most children are turned off by public school rules, regulations, irrelevant curricula, and indifferent and sometimes hostile teachers. By the time they reach the twelfth grade (given they don't drop out), they have accumulated so many negative experiences that school has become similar to a battlefield. The same holds true in some private schools where African American children are also met with resistance, insults, hostile behavior, and stereotyping by principals, teachers, and other students. It is well documented that those who teach in the public or private schools often graduate from college with little to no understanding of cultures outside their own. This creates a breeding ground for a negative teacher-student relationship that can affect students for a lifetime. Also discussed in the education chapter are alternatives to low-performing schools: home schools, faith-based schools, magnet schools, and character-building schools.

The debate over teaching Ebonics in public schools has caused a stir in the educational community. From a cultural perspective, speaking Ebonics should be as normal as humans breathing air. The problem is that Ebonics spoken outside the classroom is not given any legitimacy in Standard English classrooms. Insisting that inner-city, rural, and poor African American children speak the standard language of the dominant culture and not recognize their own devalues the youth. This essentially becomes a barrier to learning for those less assimilated than others. Today, the most popular music in the world—hip-hop—embraces and reinforces Ebonics. Moreover, most African American children hear Standard English neither at home nor in their community—they face a double whammy.

Within this work, referencing the African American child or youth/adolescent will have independent meanings. The African American child will be defined as an individual two through twelve years old, and the African American youth/adolescent will be defined as an individual thirteen through nineteen years old. The terms African American and black will be used synonymously and interchangeably.

Is the African American culture on a path towards extinction? Are African American parents and immediate caregivers preparing their children to properly function in a global technological age? These are questions that urgently need to be addressed. It is noted that African American children spend an average of seven hours a day at school. So public schools play a significant role in the socialization of this population.

Most people feel that only African Americans shape the development of black children and youth—a great misconception. Many white, Native American, Hispanic, and Asian teachers are involved in the development of African American children as well. The children spend their whole school day with educators of all races and ethnicities.

There are clear-cut examples of what sets African American children apart from other minority children during their socialization process. For example, most minority children (namely those who are economically disadvantaged) are raised in homes where Standard English is devalued and ridiculed. Historians may argue the previous statement, but no other culture on American soil has undergone such a brutal experience as African Americans—no other people have been denied their indigenous, cultural roots. However, I caution black folk on using our race as a convenient excuse to play the victim or turn away from struggle. We should feel challenged to take personal responsibility for overcoming obstacles deliberately placed in our path towards achieving success.

There are two issues that are significantly minimized in socializing African American children: bad money management and bad eating habits—both equally contributing to the plight of the black community. The lack of money-management savvy in this day and time leads to a mere existence from paycheck to paycheck and then to damaged credit, eventually affecting one's quality of life.

Poor nutritional habits lead to heart disease, strokes, and a host of other ailments that also affect the quality of one's lifestyle. Foods lacking in nutrition too often become the standard. Some practices are rooted in slavery, when the leavings of the hog were the primary seasoning, such as the fat, tails, ears, and feet.

Historically in African American culture, nutrition has been synonymous with soul food. As a people, we consume entirely too much saturated fat, sugar, starch, and salt. Although there are attempts to prepare healthier soul food, we need more emphasis on nutrition to promote better health. More African American males die of heart disease every year. This disease is preventable, yet the numbers reflect a lack of healthy dietary information and practice.

Exposing African American children to better nutrition is difficult when one considers the price of health food in comparison to that of junk food. More than half of all African American children are born into poverty, and chances are that the finances for the best nutrition will take a backseat to juggling basic household bills.

This book will also cover the generational influence in socializing African American children. From the Depression era generation to the present generation, we must consider different norms and values that are passed down to our children. Not enough parents are involved in instilling a sense of honor for community, environment, and service to others.

Overall, the desired goal for us who interact with African American young people is to become aware of our current cultural implications and hindrances, and to explore the alternatives that may effectively advance the socialization process.

CHAPTER I

Education

SOCIOLOGISTS, ANTHROPOLOGISTS AND PSYCHOLOGISTS DEFINE the socialization process as one by which children learn the rules and regulations of their own family group, their culture, and their society. "Within this framework, socialization is a process of assisting the child in acquiring the attitudes, skills, and knowledge needed to get along in that society (Harris and Liebert, 1984; McConnell, 1980)." Similarly, "Socialization also refers to the learning of information, cognitive processes, values, attitudes, social roles, self-concepts, and behaviors that are generally accepted or expected within one or many segments of American society (Berger and Luckmann, 1967; Dorr, 1982)." However, these traits in the socialization process fail to encompass values that give rise to the spiritual, communal, nonmaterial, and holistic traits that are in dire need of implementation in African American mental health.

Parents who are raising children today will most likely confirm the statement that raising them is a laborious task. Like factors that plague European American families—escalating single-parent households, high rates of drug abuse, and poverty—the African American family must also contend with blatant racism. It is the realities of systematic exclusion from mainstream resources, denial of African roots, education that discriminates against their cultural orientation or learning style, and a bombardment of negative portrayals of African American males and females in mass media. Subsequently, in the public school systems (where a significant amount of socialization occurs), the African American child

1

is not being properly trained in academics or prepared for life in the real world, which sets the stage for them suffering a myriad of problems: dysfunctional relationships, black-on-black violence, individualism, single parenthood, sentencing disparities, high rates of incarceration, breakdown in familial communication, and lack of respect for self and others. These consequential problems are often projected as being typical of the African American experience.

Oftentimes at public schools, African American children must contend with titles (not their birth names, but rather new names), such as "at risk," "special education," "dysfunctional," or "pathological." Most African American children are tagged by European, Asian, Native American, and even African American educators. Why is this so? Imposing these terms on African American children justifies pervasive tracking in the public school system. As a result, most of the lower tracking classes are filled with black youth. Children become race conscious as early as three years old. Similarly, by the time children develop their thought process, they not only become intuitively cognizant of racial differences, but they soon after become cognizant of teachers' lack of confidence in their academic skills.

Racial Socialization

RACIAL SOCIALIZATION OCCURS WHEN PARENTS attempt to prepare their children for the realities of being black in America (Taylor et al., 1990, p. 994). Parents tend to explain racial politics based on their own experiences. Another major factor in the racial socialization of the African American child depends on the era in which the parent was raised. The most profound, life-changing educational struggle most likely occurred during the civil rights era (post-1964)—the era integration was instituted.

Institutional racism transcends class and social and economic status. For that reason, most informed African American children heard similar stories from their parents that occurred during the struggle for integration. Parents of this era influenced their children's societal views with explanations of various educators' discriminatory practices. They informed their children of educators who deemed them incapable of academic learning, and even less capable of competing against white students and other students of color. And those who expressed interest in any field other than vocational education during the civil rights era were seldom encouraged, which frequently resulted in unhealthy student-teacher relations in the classroom.

African American children who are taught the social, economic and political status of blacks in this country appear better prepared than those who receive no orientation at all; for example, when encountering racism at the institutional level, these children are usually better equipped to deal with it. By the time they enter junior high, they are even better able to navigate around the pitfalls that would deter them from pursuing higher education.

As the proverb states, nothing remains the same, and life for the African American is, like racism, a fluid experience—constantly changing. Learning to cope with racism in America is a complex issue; it has and will continue to alter in its potency. Since African Americans' arrival to the northern shores in 1619, their experience has been marked by several phases of racism. Beginning in the seventeenth century through the nineteenth century, racism embodied neither social nor economic mobility; there were no advocacy organizations for literacy, and very little hope. Conversely, racism occurring in the twentieth century was characterized by a political force that resulted in the 1964 civil rights bill—the genesis of African American children entering mainstream academic institutions.

Today, parents often voice their concerns for the well-being of their children, particularly at predominantly white institutions. There are countless testimonies ascertaining that African American children feel as though school is anything but interesting or inspiring. One may wonder if this lack of interest in school is simply an epidemic among the students, or if it is a subliminal concept that is intertwined in institutional racism, which actually shortchanges both white and black youth. Although the black youth are the direct victims, they shouldn't be allowed to play the victim.

There's a lack of connection between the school curricula and the youth's world. It becomes irrelevant, a turnoff, and ultimately school becomes perceived as something that black people shouldn't aspire to—something that black people "do not do."

If institutional racism is so apparent and potent, why do African American families send their children to school? There are obvious reasons other than the law requiring it. Despite the roadblocks, parents' minimal expectation is that their children learn and master the basics: fundamental math, English, science, and reading. However, according to professors from the college community, "By year 2000 all children attending America's schools will need to know how to read, write, compute, and think clearly in order to be productive members of the workforce. The jobs will require stronger academic skills than any preceding workforce. The jobs will require an education beyond high school with almost one third requiring four or more years of college. An educated, competent workforce is becoming more essential to the nation's economic health and ability to compete internationally" (C.E. DeBose, G.T. Weddington, J.E. van Keulen 1997).These findings clearly suggest that an education from public schools that fails to satisfy the competencies above will have an excruciating effect on African American children.

Most teachers are in education, in spite of the pay, because they have a desire to teach and the institutions of higher learning produce teachers for grade school through college. However, in students' quest for meeting the criteria for becoming teachers, they inadvertently become tools of institutional racism because it's impregnated in the teaching curricula and philosophies, subsequently affecting children of all cultures, but more so African Americans.

Teachers who live in white, middle-class America may be unaware of the ramifications of emerging from a privileged world—how it affects their attempts to educate African American children. It may be more difficult for the black students in the classroom to relate to the material presented from a different viewpoint. This well-meaning teacher goes on with business as usual, never realizing that these students have made no real-world connection to the material. Educator Gary R. Howard echoes this concept as follows: "I realize that members of the dominant group in any society do not necessarily have to know anything about those people who are not like them. For our survival and the carrying on of the day-to-day activities of our lives, most white Americans do not have to engage in any meaningful personal connection with people who are different … the luxury of ignorance reinforces and perpetuates white isolation (Howard, 1999)." Teachers of a nonminority experience may fail to fully appreciate the contributions of both Africans and African Americans to world civilization.

It would be to the benefit of the whole society if cultural awareness classes were a mandatory curriculum of institutions that train the nation's teachers. Until this happens, those who graduate with no preparation for the cultural crisis in the classroom will unconsciously perpetuate institutional racism—the often unintentional imposed barriers and selection/promotion procedures, which serve to disadvantage members of minority groups.

If one were to visit most educational institutions in America, there would be one standard of cultural teaching—American white. The established concept is that the history of America begins with the Pilgrims, and black people's history begins with slavery, and when traced back further, American history looks to England—to white ancestry. And that history is supposedly accurate, negating the validity of all nonwhite people.

The impact of institutional racism imposed upon the African American child is very complex. It generally leaves them feeling alienated, ugly, devalued, powerless, rejected, and most importantly, inferior. They feel as though education is a white or Asian aspiration. Consequently, these feelings give rise to a self-destructive pattern in African American males, such as drinking, selling drugs, gang banging, stealing, and killing. For African American females, destructive behaviors—depending on age—range from promiscuity, suicide attempts, and gang activity. Teachers who witness these behaviors are often left with the impression that the African American child's problems stem solely from their immediate environment. As long as these educators remain uninformed of the effects of institutional racism, they cannot effectively teach any student, regardless of their race or ethnicity.

Per Rosalind P. Hale, strong black role models are necessary to counter the effects of institutional racism. Although Rosalind P. Hale's article refers to black women, her thoughts are very applicable to male and female African American children. When a youth has a role model from a similar class and background, it seems to foster a healthier relationship, which escalates their academic achievements. Another critical point Hale made was that by challenging them, black role models motivate the students to rise to greater heights, to become confident, never questioning their abilities. Excellence is expected and demanded by black teachers who understand the African American child's plight in the public school system. Pride, worthiness, vision, and desire to aid others are also instilled.

It is important to note that some educators claim integration at an early age may not have been the best choice for the African American child due to the seemingly lower expectations by mainstream teachers. As alluded to earlier, educators of different races are often from different communities, which may affect their understanding of the black youth's learning patterns and abilities.

Standardized achievement gaps remain a major focal point in the African American community. Indeed, standardized achievement is essential for admissions into the various modes of secondary education; that is, college, technical schools, and art schools. Many education pundits credit underperformance in standardized testing to several factors: the quality of schools, teacher training, academic curriculum, school counseling, reading habits, and parents' income and education. Certainly, underperformance on standardized testing has additional complexities other than the aforementioned. In a recent newspaper article, studies by author John U. Ogbu substantiated that middle-class black children are lagging behind their white and Asian counterparts on standardized tests, and it's even more puzzling that these middle-class African American children are from affluent suburbs, which are filled with black professionals; that is, doctors, lawyers, and teachers. Ogbu maintains that because of intense peer pressure, many African American children find it crucial to embrace and identify with what they view in movies or on television—a negative portrayal of a person of color. It is much easier for the youth to identify with the negative image with no expectations required of him or her to conform to a more positive image that will entail academic work, which may leave him or her feeling alone and unpopular. This negative attitude seems to relieve the anxiety of being labeled, "acting white."

Biculturalism: Schooling

According to the *New Webster's Dictionary and Thesaurus*, biculturalism is a state of two cultural heritages coexisting in a single social group or person. Although there are many other definitions, it can best be described as experiencing a dual socialization process. A broader definition is the process which includes mastering one's indigenous culture as well as the dominant culture—the case of the average African American child.

Without a basic understanding of self and the culture base, it is difficult for these children to buy into "the system" and understand how to make the system work for them. The bicultural socialization process requires an understanding of the African American children's native language, linguistic patterns, religion, values, beliefs, music, and history. By the time African American children graduate from high school, they should have been schooled in and have obtained a majestic knowledge of biculturalism and even tri-culturalism if they're of two different cultures. They should understand not only their own culture(s), but also the dominant or mainstream culture as well. Once African American children learn the mainstream culture, they become acculturated, which ultimately creates opportunities for mainstream American assimilation without the danger of losing their black identity. In many private or faith-centered schools, African American children assimilate within the mainstream, but lose or fail to develop their own black cultural identity in the process. This is also prevalent in public schools.

Like other children, black children whose parents possess more formal education will begin earlier in learning biculturalism. The earlier the children are exposed to a culture outside their own, the more likely they will be able to learn it and communicate within it, which is essential to success in public schools. It will also afford them better communication, upward social and economic mobility, healthier lifestyles, political literacy, and just more opportunities in general. The disadvantages of not understanding the mainstream culture result in poor communication skills, limited economic opportunities, political ignorance, and poor health. America's inner cities have become fertile ground for generations of the disadvantaged, due to isolation from the mainstream. Therefore, African American children should be versed in both black and mainstream culture—an extended version of biculturalism.

African American children are more kinesthetic and possess higher levels of motor activity (Hale, 1986, pp. 75–95). There is also compelling medical evidence that suggests that African American males have higher testosterone levels than their white counterparts. As a result, they are often misunderstood and placed in an academic climate that is counterproductive (Lattimore, 2005). This may explain the disproportionate black male dropout rate in the public school system.

The vast majority of African American children need to be socialized with people-oriented learning styles, such as group activities with teachers, peers, parents, and members of the community. To deprive them of a people-oriented learning style can be counterproductive for them.

African American children "respond best when taught in small groups with a great deal of nurturing interaction between the teacher and the child and his or her peers" (Hale, 2000, p.18). According to Janice Hale, professor of early childhood education at Wayne State University, there is a correlation between creative arts which the average African American child experiences at home and learning achievement. Hip-hop artist KRS ONE, of Boogie Down Productions, echoed this same concept in his 1990 "Edutainment" (Education + Entertainment) LP. Teaching for a people-oriented style of learning is essential for the African American child. There is ample evidence that it works, and it's simply just a practical method of learning and teaching.

Black Psychology

THERE IS STILL A PREVAILING myth in the black community that suggests striving for academic excellence is "acting white." It's even more alarming that some black adults believe this as well. Indeed, this issue has several explanations. Peer conformity and culture are the foremost determinants in the academic attitudes of black youth.

Many are convinced that people who achieve academically have an identity problem. This will almost always be the case if black role models and those with authority have not learned mainstream American culture. And since the youth tend to equate good school performance with trying to be white, in most cases, these young folk haven't been exposed to or experienced enough blacks who they are able to identify with that are pursuing academic excellence or fields of study that require excellence.

The only individuals they observe making significant progress are exceptional performing peers who they label nerdy and white people in the media, usually someone to whom black youth cannot relate. Since recent studies suggest that African American children watch more television than any other ethnic group, they accept many of its subtle messages at face value. The black youth that cannot identify with white people will frequently dismiss all academic achievement as irrelevant.

Most black adolescents frequently seek entertainers or professional athletes to identity with because they appear to possess power, glamour, and money. More often than not, other ethnic or nonethnic groups who are devalued in U.S. society tend to respond in a similar manner. This is in part why rapper Eminem, as well as other poor whites around the world gravitate towards rap music and hip-hop culture (in its 9 elements: break dancing, graffiti art, beat boxin, street fashion, language, knowledge, entrepreneurism, trade & business, MC'n/ DJ'n) KRS-ONE, 2001. Hip-hop culture in this instance serves as surrogate culture that's in line with many youths' experiences, interests, personality, and world view. In addition, there is evidence that suggest authorities in the black community willingly socialize the youth into culturally specific sports, such as baseball, basketball, and football. Academic excellence is not approached with the same vigor as athletic pursuits, especially among black males. Even if some of these aspiring athletes make it to a division one college, less than 2 percent achieve professional status.

Black males will most likely identify with a charismatic sports figure such as Alan Iverson as opposed to renowned Princeton University professor Dr. Cornel West. This is, in part, because many blacks believe that an athletic pursuit is the only democratic avenue to success that is accessible to their children. The people who influence them the most, their parents, ultimately pass down this attitude from generation to generation.

One proactive measure that parents and immediate caregivers could take is to expose their children to successful black role models who pursued academic excellence and are living productive lifestyles. For example, Barack Obama (the first African American U.S. President) has served as an example to the African American community and the world that dedication, education, and hard work are critical for success. Introducing one's children to black history is another effective method to motivate academic excellence.

U.S. Educational System's International Ranking

IN COMPARISON TO OTHER COUNTRIES in the international educational rankings, America fares very poorly. According to the United Nations, the United States is ranked eighteenth out of twenty-two developed nations surveyed by the United Nations Children's Fund (UNICEF). Research revealed that most of America's problems with its youth originate from the home and not in the classroom. In fact, a child's socioeconomic status and the educational level of his or her parents were significant factors.

This study was premised upon five diverse tests of fourteen- and fifteen-year-olds that gauged their math, reading, and science proficiency (See Table 1.1). In addition, the study averaged the results to render "the most comprehensive picture to date of how well each nation's education system is functioning as a whole," UNICEF said.

Table 1.1 World Education Rankings

1. South Korea	9. Sweden	18. United States *
2. Japan	10. Czech Republic –	19. Germany-(tie)
3. Finland	(tie) New Zealand	Denmark
4. Canada	12. France	21. Spain
5. Australia	13. Switzerland	22. Italy
6. Austria	14. Belgium –(tie)	23. Greece
7. Britain	Iceland	24. Portugal
8. Ireland	16.. Hungary-(tie)	
	Norway	

Source: UNICEF

According to the Brookings Institution and the Higher Education Research Institute, "Only a third of high school seniors in the United States report spending more than five hours a week on homework." This is contrary to their international peers. International high school students tend to have more homework and thus spend more time on homework. There was no time frame given in the study.

In addition, there is a debate among parents, students, and educators about how much homework is sufficient. It is evident that U.S. students are not faring as well as their international counterparts. The study by the Brookings Institution and the Higher Education Research Institute suggests that U.S. students spend more time socializing, working for pay, and playing sports than studying and doing homework. Also, U.S. students placed more importance on the following: watching television, partying, and participating in student clubs or groups. These factors affect African American youth and others in an even more alarming manner. First, African American youth, disadvantaged poor Caucasian youth, and other minorities grapple with the barrier of disconnection from the mainstream education and educator. Second, these populations are often doing homework assignments without support from their parents, which could affect their ranking with their international peers. Based on this study, more relevant homework coupled with more studying will create better students. The following study suggests that United States students typically do no more than an hour of homework a day along with spending less time on take-home assignments than their international peers (See Table 1.2).

Table 1.2 Homework Ranks behind Other Pursuits

Socializing with friends, 75.8 %

Working (for pay), 58.3%

Exercising/playing sports, 49.9%

Studying/homework, 33.4%

Watching TV, 26%

Partying, 25.1%

Participating in student clubs/groups 14%

Source: Brookings Institution and Higher Education Research Institute

Although the U.S. education ranking in the world is low, parents and immediate caregivers can become proactive by arranging tutoring for their children. They must not only reinforce what their children are learning at school, they must also set aside time to visit with schoolteachers and tutors to ensure academic success. Results of full-time academics, intensive tutoring, and limited socializing can be noted in South Korea, Japan, and Finland's higher world-education rankings—all above that of the United States. One of the United States' greatest resources should be their properly educated children.

Behavioral Disparities as Early as Kindergarten

African American children's behavioral differences may be a contributing factor to their poor cognitive skills, according to researchers. Moreover, researchers' data may also prove valid in explaining why African American children tend to be less prepared to adjust to the behavioral demands of school. According to the National Center for Education Statistics, in 1998, a kindergarten survey required teachers to answer three questions about their students: (1) whether they persisted at the tasks assigned to them; (2) whether they were eager to learn new things; and (3) whether they regularly paid attention in class. The findings of this study concluded that, in comparison to white and Hispanic children, black children exhibited less persistence at school tasks, demonstrated less ambition to master new things, and were less attentive in the classroom. (See Figure 1.1., below.)

Figure 1-1. Percentage of Kindergartners Rated by as "Never" or Only "Sometimes" Behaving in Ways Conducive to Learning, 1998

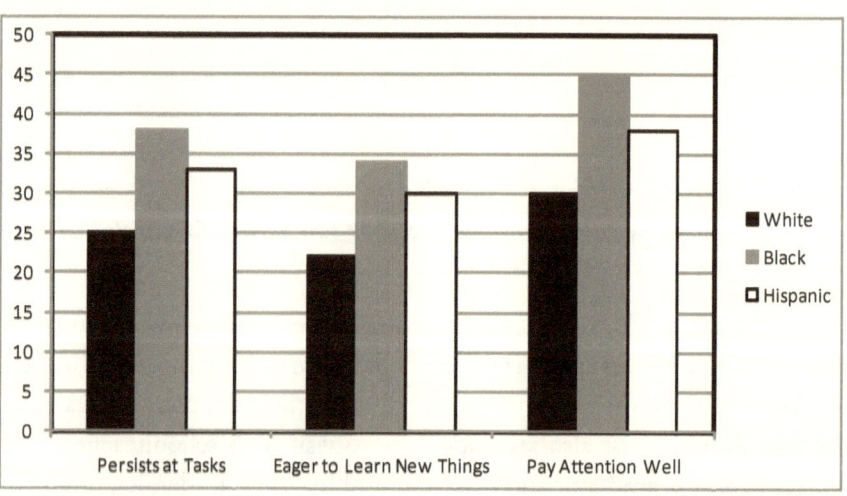

Source: National Center for Education Statistics, America's Kindergartners, 30, 47.

In addition, teachers reported that African American students in kindergarten were inclined to engage in verbal and physical aggression with their peers. Only if the assessment of these teachers is accurate, could one make the case of a correlation between racial differences and meeting expectations of schools. This study also revealed that single parents consider their own children to be hyperactive and easily distracted, confirming survey and educators' conclusions.

In light of this suggestion, children—namely African American—who live with one parent could fall behind others in the following areas: their ability to persist at a task; ambition to master new tasks, and ability to focus during class; they may be more likely to display argumentative and physically aggressive behaviors.

Single parents frequently complain of the arduous task of working two jobs to "barely get by," and of problems mustering the energy to discipline their children. This is the reason extended or surrogate families are so important. However, if a single African American mother lacks a support system, her children could suffer from a lack of discipline. For example, the following scenario between Nikki and Carmen is an example of nonquality, extended family kinships.

Nikki is a twenty-five-year-old, single mother of two. She works as a customer service representative. On weekends, she babysits for twenty-four-year-old Carmen, a single mother, who works as a nursing assistant during the week so that she can complete her bachelor's degree on the weekends. Nikki and Carmen became friends through a mutual friend at their church. Nikki volunteers her babysitting services most of the time, and to Carmen, this deal is irresistible. However, due to Carmen's workload and life obstacles, she's frequently exhausted, and often doesn't have the energy to properly discipline her child. Similarly, when Carmen's five-year-old son is with Nikki, who shoulders the same responsibilities as Carmen, very little effort is placed on discipline for many of the same frustrations and reasons.

It is important to note that this is not always the case, but it occurs more often than not; discipline is moved to the back burner in these situations. In contrast, the scenario below is an example of a quality extended-family kinship.

JoAnn is a twenty-six-year-old, single mother of one. Her occupation is a retail store manager. During her evening shifts, JoAnn is in need of a babysitter that she can trust. She decided to call Karen, a longtime friend, a twenty-seven-year-old, single parent who works as an executive assistant. JoAnn has always perceived Karen as a good communicator, and as responsible and firm with her two children. Karen consented on the following conditions: they would use joint rule setting, consequences would be jointly defined, and positive reinforcement would be equally agreed upon for good behavior. Karen balances work and parenting by relying on her brother and first cousin to look after her two children when she is at work. She makes sure her extended family reinforces the same discipline her children receive at home. Karen, no matter how tired she becomes, places a premium on discipline and considers it as the cornerstone to developing successful children.

The Four-Year Skills Gap

THE NATIONAL ASSESSMENT OF EDUCATIONAL Progress (NAEP), more commonly known as "the nation's report card," pioneered by Congress in 1969, regularly tests nationally representative samples of America's elementary and secondary school students in the fourth, eighth, and twelfth grades, or sometimes at ages nine, thirteen, and seventeen.(Thernstrom, 2003).

The most recent results of the NAEP systematically reveal an alarming gap between the basic academic skills of the average black, Hispanic, white, and Asian student. More specifically, NAEP findings suggest that at the twelfth grade, the average African American student lags four years behind his or her white and Asian counterparts. Hispanics were reported as not faring much better. Figure 1-2 displays the results of the most recent NAEP tests in four core subjects. These data are disturbing because those who fail to master fundamental intellectual skills and lifestyles will be limited today and tomorrow.

Figure 1-2. The Four-Year Gap: How Black and Hispanic High School Seniors Perform Compared to Whites and Asians in the 8th Grade

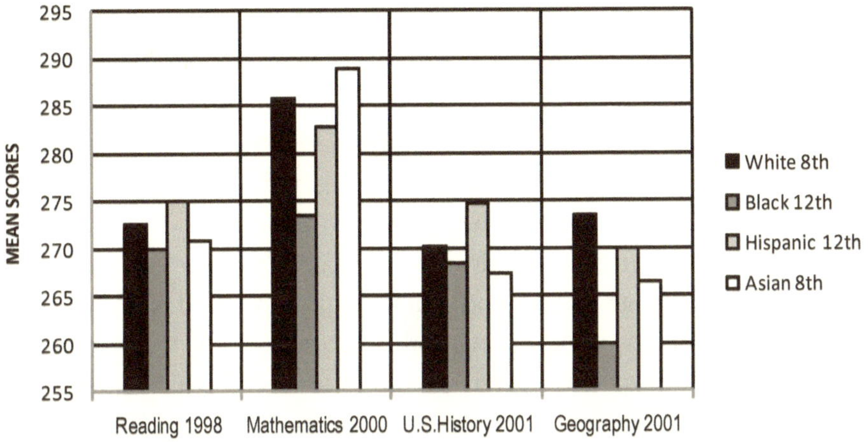

Source: National Assessment for Educational Progress Data Tool.

Most African American parents regard the current public educational system as a failure. So-called steps that have been taken by President George W. Bush have placed educational reform as a priority of his domestic agenda (Thernstrom, 2003). Regardless of the current leadership's approach to remedy the issue, the four-year skills gap is not improving.

The more dismaying fact is that African American youth will one day have to compete for a job in an already fierce global job market. The would-be employers of various companies and institutions automatically assume that individuals with high school diplomas can read complex material, write reasonably well, and perform basic math calculations. However, due to so many students slipping through the cracks, our postindustrial, information-based workforce consists of high school graduates functioning on an sixth- to eighth-grade skills level—namely African Americans, Hispanics, and poor whites.

One must bear in mind that in all racial groups, there are some who do exceptionally well in core subjects such as reading, mathematics, U.S. history, and geography. Whites represent 60 percent of the nation's schoolchildren, while blacks and Latinos are a little less than one-third combined (Thernstrom, 2003).

Below Basic

BELOW BASIC IS A TERM that essentially describes a student's inability to demonstrate partial mastery of prerequisite knowledge and skills that are essential for proficient work at their grade level. However, an overwhelming number of American students across both racial and social class lines, according to the NAEP, are graduating from high school with academic skills that are below basic. In fact, in reading and writing alone, nearly one-quarter of all students are below basic in these areas. These are two skills that are essential in admissions to vocational school and college. Similarly, in math, geography, and civics, roughly one-third of all students were below basic levels. According to this information, African American parents and immediate caregivers should raise several critical questions: (1) Were the NAEP achievement levels set too high? (2) What is the standard of teaching in public schools? (3) Does the board of education hold anyone accountable for graduating students who fall below basic? (4) And most importantly, what is the goal of public school education?

Prior to African American children entering public school, their self-concept is usually healthy. They've absorbed information that relates to their community and reality; they're eager to learn more; they are open to new ideas; and most importantly, they are unafraid to dream big. However, it has been well documented that African American children lose these qualities as early as third or fourth grade. Rather than enhancing the skills and attitudes they began school with, they gradually lose interest in school, and despise it along with themselves, thereby becoming emotionally and intellectually crippled.

Some of the contributing factors to this problem are unqualified teachers and integrated school systems, which include low expectations and no mentorship for these children. By the time the youths reach twelfth grade (if they remain in school), they suffer from a broken spirit. Thus a generation of underachievers and nonbelievers are created. From a domestic and international perspective, African American children and adolescents will continue to lag behind other cultures and countries if they continue their current rate of progress.

A very pertinent factor in preparing black children for success within the school system or in life is the need to listen to them. Their curiosity should be satisfied by seriously considering and answering their questions. Parents should encourage them to discuss their hopes, dreams, and fears, no matter how big or small.

It's equally important to assist children with difficult homework assignments, always challenging them to do their best. Parents should accompany their children to the library, read to them and play books on tapes and CDs, and share more educational television programs with them. The education process cannot be the sole responsibility of the school system.

Socializing African American children, through primary education in the twenty-first century, should behoove parents to stop waiting to be rescued by the government and to take responsibility for their children's future. There's a need for less talk and more creative action from parents and others who are dissatisfied with the current public educational system.

Both African American educators and parents in general have voiced concerns to authorities for public schools to be held accountable and to deliver a quality education to the children. Many folks believed that the "No Child Left Behind Act," which sets national accountability standards for schools allotted federal funding, would be the answer to the educational crisis in public education. Contrary to popular belief, the 2001 act failed to turn around low-performance public schools. In addition, black mayors across the country maintain that the act holds poorly funded schools in impoverished cities to the same standards as the schools with more generous funding. The bottom line is that lower-funded education and public school systems are not producing equitable results as those better-funded schools.

Homeschooling

IN RESPONSE TO THE EDUCATIONAL crisis in public schools, middle-class African American parents are teaching their children in the home. The surge in homeschooling has become increasingly more common in the twenty-first century, primarily as an alternative to public school. According to the National Home Education Research Institute (NHERI), since 1990, the number of homeschooled children in the country has soared, increasing by 400 percent, which equals about 2 million students. Currently, there are approximately 9.5 million African Americans enrolled in schools. Of this figure, 120,000 children are homeschooled. Since late 1997-2003, homeschooling among African American students has risen from 1 percent to 5 percent (Jonsson, 2003). This surge in homeschooling among African American students is largely due to a failing public educational system. Therefore, parents deem homeschooling as a viable option to public school.

The curriculum English, math, science, and foreign language are subjects equivalent to public school, but parents often provide more field trips which afford the student hands-on experiences. This accelerated learning process appears to pique student's interest more than the writing and reading process. Education comes to life—to full circle.

State laws mandate parents who teach their children at home to follow curriculum guidelines, and they're happy to comply. They have compelling reasons for educating their children themselves. The main justification is that the environment is controlled—it's more conducive to learning. The parent's moral or religious values remain intact is another factor that has played a role in the surge of homeschooling. In fact, approximately two-thirds of the homeschooled populations are children of devout Christians and Jews who are outraged with the public school systems' immorality and a seeming lack of dedication and values. Furthermore, African American parents cite poor instruction, low student achievement, lack of safety, a lack of individual attention, a lack of racial pride, and a lack of cultural diversity in the curriculum as rationales for homeschooling. As a result of the lack of connectivity to the subject material, as previously discussed, African American males in primary school are in a serious plight. They are often trapped in remedial or special education courses that bring with them a stereotype and a negative self-concept that many never escape; they often carry it the remainder of their lives.

African American males in primary school are much less likely to be placed in gifted and talented courses or the advanced placements for exceptional children. Given this plight of African American males in primary school, it is a relief to witness this alternative course of action: homeschooling.

There are a few in the field of education that are passionately opposed to homeschooling. Such foes argue that African American students who undergo a homeschooling regimen are not afforded the same high academic standards as students in public school. In fact, some make the argument that homeschooling undermines the civil-rights struggle that won all Americans equal access to public schools.

According to statistician Lawrence Ludner of the University of Maryland, test scores from twenty thousand homeschooled children were significantly higher on standardized tests than the national average (Wooster, 2000). Similarly, in a fifteen-year study conducted by the National Home Education Research Institute, homeschooled children scored fifteen to thirty points above the national average. Therefore, as a general rule, homeschooling is a valid and successful alternative to the flagging public school system.

School Choice

SIMILAR TO HOMESCHOOLING, GRANTING PARENTS the option of transferring children to different schools was another necessary alternative to the failing public schooling systems. According to Mary Lord, school choice provides parents with alternatives of placing their children in high-performance educational systems. More specifically, school choice allows African American parents to send their kids to magnet programs, single-sex academies, or independently run charter schools, using tuition vouchers for private or religious schools or educating children at home.

The results of these educational alternatives have proved to be promising. In single-sex public schools, research suggests that girls perform better as a result of no distractions from boys. "Black male students who thrive in these single-gender academic settings often have demonstrated higher test scores, graduation rates and acceptance into college than their public school counterparts (English, 2006)."Moreover, single-sex classes have the potential of catering to several learning styles and cognitive development particular to either boys or girls. Parents frequently express their satisfaction with the schools' faculty concerns for college preparation. Unlike regular public school systems, single-sex public schools impose a no-nonsense, rigorous curriculum, which requires advanced placement courses as early as seventh grade. Indeed single-sex schools have a track record of developing students into successful adults.

African American parents who desire to take a hands-on approach to their child's education can do so by enrolling their child in a charter school. In a recent article, a mother of two chose this alternative school because of two attractive qualities: the school's emphasis on hands-on projects and the semester-long themes, such as agriculture and politics.

The Notion of Educational Equality

CURRENT RESEARCH SUGGESTS THAT OVER half of black youths reside in homes of single-parent families, typically headed by women. Therefore, black women are usually the primary socializers of the African American children, and many do not include the public school system as a viable alternative for their children's education. They feel that their children will not have the same opportunities as children in white suburbia. Many two-parent families struggle with the same thought. The following scenario explores this idea further.

Donna is a forty-year-old college professor of engineering. She lives with her husband, Chauncy, who works as a foreman at a plastic manufacturer in a suburb in Virginia. Donna and her husband decided that they did not want Malcolm, their nine-year-old, to continue his education in a public school. More importantly, the couple felt that placing their nine-year-old son in an academic climate at a predominately white institution would afford their son a better opportunity. Donna and Chauncy made a conscious effort not to discuss overt racism that he would encounter in school and throughout society. When questioned about this choice, they replied, "We don't want Malcolm growing up with an inferiority complex. We want him to feel that he can achieve regardless of his color." They felt that the best method of accomplishing this was to place him in a different learning environment that they felt was superior.

African American parents who confront extensive challenges to position their children in affluent school districts are confronted with a possibly denigrating trade-off as well. According to John (Ogbu, 2003), who has done groundbreaking research regarding the underachievement of black children in affluent suburbs on a national level, the educational levels of white children and black children are acutely polarized, with white children faring better. Moreover, often black children are encouraged by teachers or counselors to enroll in easier, general education courses and no college preparatory courses. Also, African American children entering affluent suburban schools are often subjected to racism and experience underachievement.

Black parents should seriously consider homeschooling or same-sex or same-race schools as viable alternatives to the current educational system. Some parents may argue about the cost of specialized education, but if enough parents and concerned citizens pool their resources, specialized education can become a realistic goal. The black church has the capacity to spearhead this reform. Many churches that are able to generate the finances include a pool of talented educators who desire to create relevant ministries for the community.

CHAPTER 2

———➤ ◄———

Nutrition/Health

LIVING IN A FAST-PACED MARKET-DRIVEN culture has catapulted African Americans to declining diet and health lifestyles. Traditions that involve the entire family sitting at the table for a nutritious meal are vanishing. Prior to 1976, childhood obesity was not an issue. Now childhood obesity is an epidemic; it is also a contributor to type II diabetes in children.

Far too many African American parents and caregivers set bad eating habits for their children. However, nutritional information can be very misleading; there is conflicting information on nutritional values of certain foods and supplements. A prime example is the controversy regarding chocolate. Now it's considered a food with high antioxidant properties (anti-cancer, anti-aging), but it has a high refined sugar content. The pro messages suggest that only dark chocolate has antioxidant properties, but due to the sugar content, one should limit its consumption. Parents will need to study nutritional information, including reading labels and drawing their own conclusions.

Foods that were rich in essential vitamins once harvested by local farmers are today replaced by foods from corporate farms. Multimillionaire corporations tend to compromise nutritional value in foods such as fruits and vegetables for greater profits. The use of artificial hormones, insecticides, and pesticides in produce and livestock feed is commonplace.

Purchasing organically grown food is a guarantee of healthy produce, but, for a single black male or female that is raising children, purchasing higher-priced organic food is not a priority—not an option. As an alternative to expensive organic food, it would be most beneficial to raise a garden, even if the produce is grown in pots on a patio or terrace. However, cheap and genetically altered foods are not the only contributors to a declining healthy lifestyle among them. These youngsters also learn self-medicating habits such as over-eating in an attempt to cope with emotional despair.

African American children who are raised in households where their parents battle emotional scars—common for some single black women— may be at a higher risk of being deprived of proper nutrition. According to Boyd, a clinical psychotherapist, "About six out of every ten black women in this country suffer from some type of major physical disorder related to their emotional well-being" (Boyd, 1993, p. 101). As a result, many black women are experiencing health problems such as obesity, anorexia, hypertension, heart disease, diabetes, headaches, cancer, alcoholism, and drug addiction. They could have been victims of physical, verbal, or sexual abuse. Add the emotional scars to poor nutritional habits, and the denial of their physical or emotional abuse background, equals black women who are physically and emotionally abusing their bodies, thereby setting health-threatening examples for their children.

According to Charlene Akers (2000), television has been cited as the number one cause of childhood and adolescent obesity: it replaces physical activity. Equally important, experts agree that the resulting lack of physical activity is the primary reason kids become overweight. Twenty years ago, parents would send their children outside after school, where they'd play games or climb trees until dinnertime. African American children today, who consume more hours of television than any other ethnic-minority group, fall prey to more appealing junk food commercials than children fifteen years ago. Thus, many African American children have replaced eating fruits and vegetables, drinking water, and playing hopscotch, marble shooting, and bike riding for eating cookies and chips, drinking soda, and playing video games and watching television shows.

Health researchers suggest that during the period between 1976 and 1980, 15 percent of adolescents ages twelve to nineteen were overweight. More current studies taken from 1988–1991 revealed figures that show childhood obesity had increased from 21 percent to 40 percent. In addition, "Between 1980 and 1994, the number of obese children in the

United States almost doubled, with nearly 14 percent of all children six to eleven, now considered overweight" (Akers, 2000, p.52). However, child obesity is becoming an epidemic worldwide. In fact, the researchers declare that 25 percent of American children, 16 percent of Russian children, and 7 percent of Chinese children ages six to eighteen are either overweight or obese. It's imperative for African American parents and immediate caregivers to understand that excessive body fat in children gives rise to heart disease and diabetes (Hope, 2002).

Psychological Causes of Overeating

HEALTH PROFESSIONALS OF THE MENTAL health community tend to agree that the overindulgence in food is linked to complex issues aside from willpower. In fact, mental health professionals believe that compulsive eaters attempt to cope with emotions such as anger, fear, boredom, and sadness. This behavior is typically learned in childhood during the times when parents and teachers may reward behaviors with junk food. Parents of African American children who lack the proper education on nutrition pass this value on to their children, and the value in turn becomes ingrained into African American culture. Also, unchecked obesity in children often leads to low self-esteem, which is discussed further in the chapter on self-esteem.

Fundamentals of Nutrition

ONE OF THE MOST UNDERRATED issues is the relationship between nutrition/ health and the socialization process. Some parents fail to understand the significance of teaching poor dietary habits, especially since the African American culture embraces its current eating trends as normal or okay (Villarosa, 1994). Most problems must be properly assessed before a correct solution can be prescribed. The link between good health and nutrition must be understood by the entire African American community.

Since black youth learn their eating habits from those who have the most influence on them—their parents—the youth innocently observe them preparing meals that are often referred to as soul food, which are usually high in fat, cholesterol, sugar, and salt. Ingredients found in most black cuisine trigger escalating ailments such as type II diabetes, a disease that once struck mostly the middle-aged but is now becoming more prevalent among adolescents. According to Dr. James R. Gavin, "Blacks comprise about 2.8 million of the nation's diabetics and are 1.7 times more likely to have the disease than whites" (*Jet*, July 2002, p. 20). African Americans, like other Americans, are obsessed with what tastes good to them as opposed to what is good for them.

Health and Success

RECENT RESEARCH FROM THE CENTERS for Disease Control and Prevention (CDC) confirms that most African American diets are unbalanced. Meanwhile, most children have a general idea of a career choice when they grow up: a fireman, lawyer, basketball player, teacher, business owner, or singer. It's the adults' role to encourage these ambitions, but the link between health, education, and professional achievement is seldom considered. Far too many operate as though there is no connection at all.

According to the CDC, overweight children are being hospitalized at escalating rates for diabetes and other diseases triggered by obesity. Hypothetically speaking, if African American children are experiencing degenerative health problems at an early age, their dreams may never be realized.

Milk: Does It Do a Body Good?

AFRICAN AMERICAN YOUTH LIVING IN today's market-driven world have been inundated by the slogan, "Milk, it does a body good." Viewers who read this catchy phrase, without contrary information, will most likely take it to heart. The problem for African Americans, and other people across the racial divide, is that many can't digest milk or milk-based products. According to the Journal of the American College of Nutrition, about 70 percent of African Americans are lactose intolerant, a physical condition in which people cannot digest lactose-bearing dairy products.

Lactose is a large sugar molecule found in milk products, and lactose intolerance is a condition that occurs in individuals who were born without, or have lost, the digestive enzyme which allows one to digest most dairy products containing the sugar molecule. Symptoms of lactose intolerance include gas, cramps, bloating, and diarrhea. Kent DeLong, MD (1992), suggests that lactose intolerance varies with each ethnic group (See Table 2.1)

Table 2.1- The prevalence of lactose intolerance in adults of certain ethnic groups:

Ethnic Group	Percent Intolerance
African blacks	95%
Indian	90%
Asian	90%
North American blacks	75%
Mexican Americans	75%
Mediterranean	60%
North American whites	15%

Given these statistics, people of African descent should be concerned about methods of combating this condition. Many African Americans who choose to avoid milk and milk products do so by substituting soy- and rice-based products. Soy products are optimal as an alternative for milk products because they're easier to digest and have similar nutritional properties to cow's milk. These products can be purchased at almost any supermarket at a reasonable price. Goats' milk is another good alternative— it's very digestible, and its composition is similar to human milk.

Fear No Fiber

THE AVERAGE AFRICAN AMERICAN ADULT'S diet lacks sufficient fiber; consequently, their children, especially those who consume excessive junk food, suffer. Fiber is nature's internal body sweeper and is necessary for optimal health—which is sacrificed when fast foods and packaged foods are consumed.

There are two types of fiber: soluble fiber and insoluble fiber. Soluble fiber dissolves in water; insoluble fiber cannot. For example, foods that contain soluble fiber are oats, oat bran, seeds, brown rice, dried beans and peas, barley, and vegetables such as carrots, corn, cauliflower, and sweet potatoes, and fruits such as apples, strawberries, oranges, bananas, nectarines, and pears. Moreover, soluble fiber helps regular body weight due to its low calorie filling effect in the stomach. Insoluble fiber is found in wheat bran, corn bran, whole-wheat breads and cereals, vegetables such as potatoes with skin, parsnips, green beans, and broccoli, and some fruits. This fiber also helps push waste through the digestive system (Matthew, K. and Pratt, G.S., 2006).

Fiber found in carbohydrates, commonly referred to as roughage, is plant-cell material that's only partially broken down during digestion. African American parents need to understand the significance of the three disease-fighting properties found in complex carbohydrates: fiber, antioxidant vitamins, and minerals.

Consuming foods that are rich in complex carbohydrates affects the body by allowing the small intestine to absorb the nutrients from food, and then pass only the bulky fiber to the large intestine. In the large intestine, the fiber absorbs water and is ultimately expelled. Parents or immediate caregivers tend to negate this important natural process by purchasing foods that are convenient and without proper nutrition. Consequently, instead of eating high-fiber foods, which aid the digestive system in the passing of toxins through the bowels, parents purchase junk food, which is proven to hinder regular bowels, contribute to obesity, and give rise to the onset of cancer.

Fiber supplements are no substitute for vegetables or fruit or whole-grain foods. Most supplements are water soluble, which means that the body is only able to retain 10 to 15 percent of their nutrition; therefore, it's imperative to eat naturally fiber-rich foods.

Teenagers

DURING THE ADOLESCENT YEARS, WHEN the youth's body is developing in spurts, there is an increased need for nutrition. Many parents find it increasingly difficult to train their children to eat nutritionally, and part of the problem stems from African American children viewing too much television—more than any other ethnic group in the United States. During this period, African American parents witness the fast-food industry undermining their wholesome eating strategies.

Black girls and boys possess similar and diverse nutritional needs. The females, like their male counterparts, should consume a diet as close to including four major food groups (meats, vegetables, fruits, breads) as possible. With the exception of dairy products, additional items on the food pyramid are essential. Above all, parents should monitor adolescent intake of protein, calcium, iron, and fruits and vegetables. For instance, female adolescents who consume excessive protein will not develop more muscle, but rather more fat (McCarthy, 2002). Females usually require approximately 1,300 mg of calcium daily, which equals a cup of cow's milk or the equivalent or a six-ounce container of yogurt (about 300 mg). "Girls especially are prone to be calcium deficient throughout the teen years, largely because milk, the single best source of calcium, is so often shunned as fattening" (McCarthy, 2002,). For those who are lactose-intolerant or vegetarian, additional sources of calcium can be found in the following: precipitated tofu, canned salmon, sardines that contain the bones, broccoli, beans, and bean sprouts.

Parents must set the stage for African American children to learn proper nutrition and disease control measures.

Creating Prostate Cancer Awareness and Prevention for Young Males

BREAST CANCER AWARENESS IS MORE visible in the community than prostate cancer awareness, which often leaves the adolescent black male oblivious of a ravaging disease that can be possibly prevented with nutritious high-fiber foods.

According to The World Health Organization (2009), prostate cancer is the second leading cause of cancer deaths in men. In a recent report by the CDC, heart disease is cited as the number one cause of death for African American men. Nutrition pundits have linked certain cancers, such as prostate, to the dietary mineral selenium, a powerful antioxidant that protects against serious diseases, including cancer. It also triggers vitamin E activity in the body and aids the body in reserving its vitamin E storage.

LeWine maintains, in a 2008 article published in the South Florida Sun-Sentinal, that rather than taking the lycopene supplements, one should eat foods rich in lycopene such as tomatoes to help prevent prostate cancer. Moreover, foods such as green leafy vegetables and fruits rich in vitamin D were noted as foods that may decrease risk of prostate cancer.

Furthermore, research suggests that selenium not only helps to prevent cancer, it also helps eliminate cancer after it develops. Plus selenium doesn't harm normal prostates or other normal human cells. Also, selenium protects good fats, DNA, and protein in the body from oxidative damage.

Parents and caregivers of African American youth have the option of acquiring selenium from supplements or through foods. Adults require a 200 microgram (mcg) dosage on a daily basis. Anything that surpasses this level is deemed toxic (see selenium information). Selenium supplements can be purchased at any health food center. Selenomethionine and high-selenium yeast are also excellent supplements and are recommended by many nutritionists.

It is not necessary to introduce selenium supplements to African American youth until their adult years (age eighteen and over). The youth can acquire their selenium by eating selenium-rich foods, such as bran, garlic from selenium-rich soil, oatmeal, onions, mushrooms, broccoli, brown rice, and whole-grain products. Other foods that contain selenium are eggs, tuna, seafood, chicken, and liver. It's important to note that low soil levels of selenium and food processing contribute to acquiring insufficient amounts in the diet (Challem and Brown, (2002), pp. 61–62).

Black children should be made aware of cancer prevention strategies by beginning their diet with antioxidants such as vitamin C, vitamin E, and beta-carotene, found in most yellow and orange vegetables and fruits (pumpkins, peppers, carrots, sweet potatoes, and cantaloupe).

According to Barbara Dixon, "Antioxidants protect healthy cells from damaging molecules known as free radicals, present in our environment. Air pollution and food additives are known as free radicals. These unstable molecules travel through the body, oxidize everything they touch and cause mutations in cells and damage to DNA" (Dixon, 1994, p. 13). Due to this damage, people, including children, are more susceptible to cancer. The later children are introduced to junk foods, the better chance good eating habits can be established and the better chance they have at eating nutritionally as adults, thereby delaying or preventing the onset of degenerative diseases.

Vegetarians

AFRICAN AMERICAN PARENTS AND CAREGIVERS who are vegetarians will most likely raise their children with a similar belief system. A vegetarian's diet consists of four basic food groups: grains, legumes, fruit, and vegetables. There are three types of vegetarians:

1. Ovo-lacto-vegetarians. They do not eat any animal flesh but do use dairy products and eggs.

2. Lacto-vegetarians. They do not eat any animal flesh or eggs but do use dairy products.

3. Vegans. They do not eat animals products of any type, including animal flesh (red meat, chicken, pork, fish, or shellfish), dairy products, eggs, or honey.

There has been a surprisingly increase of vegetarian diets among teenagers. Adolescents are straying away from meat diets as a result of environmental or animal rights issues (Amy Lanou, 2002, p. 88).

Additionally, children appear to benefit more from a vegetarian lifestyle. In general, these children were found to be leaner; on average, vegetarians are 10 percent leaner than omnivores. This places those who are physically fit at a significant advantage. For instance, African American youth who are not obese lessen the risk of the onset of degenerative diseases. A healthy heart is the most outstanding. Vegetarians tend to have lower cholesterol levels than nonvegetarians. Vegans have even lower levels. Moreover, "Vegetarians are about 40 percent less likely to get cancer than nonvegetarians, regardless of other risks such as smoking, body size, and socioeconomic status" (Lanou, 2002, p. 7). This is partly due to vegetarians' meatless, egg-free, and dairy-free diets—foods that have been associated with cancer. Recent studies indicate that naturally occurring compounds in vegetables, such as beta-carotene, lycopene, folic acid, and genistein, are instrumental in warding off cancer. In addition, ingesting natural antioxidants found in fruits and some vegetables appears to help prevent and restore cell damage.

Overall good health, normal blood pressure, and a lower risk of diabetes are other benefits of vegetarianism. Meat eaters tend to have higher blood pressure than non–meat eaters. Among a group of African Americans, a study found high blood pressure in 44 percent of nonvegetarians, but in only 18 percent of vegetarians.

Juvenile-onset diabetes is escalating at alarming rates, particularly type II diabetes. Vegetarians, whose diet consists of the new four food groups, play a significant role in reducing diabetes in African American youth. In fact, vegetarianism not only lessens the chances of diabetes, adhering to a vegetarian diet has also reversed the effects of type II diabetes, even in adults (Lanou, 2002, p. 8).

Weight Gain

ALTHOUGH IT'S DETRIMENTAL TO THEIR health, at least one in three black youth has an acquaintance that is able to eat several servings of fattening foods—pizzas, pastries, chips and dips, or malts—without gaining weight. All too often, these peers of female black youth who possess prized physical attributes such as a slender build and attractive facial features become the standard to which other black females aspire. Per authors Paul A. Jones, MD, and Angela Mitchell (2002), genetics, individual metabolism, and a slew of other factors combine to determine a person's propensity to gain or lose weight. Many young people will have to understand they can't mimic others' eating habits.

In order to lose weight, youngsters must burn off more calories than they consume. Although fruits, vegetables, and grains are deemed optimal for proper nutrition, they can cause weight gain if more calories are consumed than burned (Jones and Mitchell, (2002), p. 129). Several determinants must be considered, such as age, weight, and level of exercise, in order to assess each child's caloric and energy needs, which will ultimately control their weight.

Moreover, one's choice of food is as important as the amount one consumes. For instance, if two children eat identical portions of food, but one child eats 60 percent of his food in the form of complex carbohydrates and the other ingests his calories from mostly fat, the two bodies will react differently. Complex carbohydrates, unlike fats, have a low probability of being stored in adipose tissue (connective tissue that functions as the major fat storage site). Studies conducted at the University of Massachusetts Medical School indicate that consuming one hundred extra carbohydrate calories will result in twenty-three of those calories being used in the food process and digestion and seventy-seven of those calories being stored as fat.

Table 2.2. Healthy Choices for Vending Machines

Instead of	Suggest
1. Potato chips	Baked tortilla chips
2. Artificially flavored and colored corn/cheese snacks	Popcorn
3. Candy bars	Granola bars; trail mix
4. Sweetened, fruit-flavored roll-ups	Fruits, dried or fresh
5. Fruit-flavored drinks with added sugar; soda pop	Water; unsweetened 100% juices
6. Whole milk; full-fat yogurt	Skim or low-fat milk, and yogurt
7. Ice cream	Sherbet or popsicles
8. Creme-filled sandwich cookies; chocolate-chip cookies	Fig bar cookies; graham crackers

The following table highlights the excessive calorie and fat content found in fast food. The reader should note that 4 grams of fat is equal to 1 teaspoon of shortening. While trans, saturated fats and cholesterol are the unhealthy fats, polyunsaturated and monounsaturated are the healthier choices of fat. On average a child (4 to 18) only needs 20-23% fat in their total (2000 daily) calorie intake according to the Center for Disease Control and Prevention (2009).

Table 2.3 Fast Food

FAST FOOD

MCDONALD'S

POOR CHOICE	MAYBE	BETTER CHOICE
Big Mac	Quarter Pounder	Grilled Chicken Deluxe
560 calories + 31 g fat	420 calories + 21 g fat (w/o mayo)	300 calories + 5 g fat
Chicken McNuggets (9)	Cheeseburger	Hamburger
430 calories + 26 g fat	320 calories + (?) g fat	260 calories + 9 g fat
		Grilled Chicken Salad
Large French Fries	Small French Fries	(with fat-free dressing)
450 calories + 22 g fat	210 calories + 10 g fat	120 calories + 1.5 g fat
Sausage Biscuit	Egg McMuffin	Hotcakes
470 calories + 31 g fat	290 calories + 12 g fat	340 calories + 9 g fat
		Low-Fat Apple
Cheese Danish	Cinnamon Roll	Bran Muffin
410 calories + 22 g fat	390 calories + 16 g fat	300 calories + 3 g fat

BURGER KING

DEADLY	MAYBE	BETTER CHOICE
Whopper with Cheese	Whopper Jr. (without mayo)	BK Broiler (without mayo)
760 calories + 48 g fat	320 calories + 15 g fat	370 calories + 9 g fat

WENDY'S

DEADLY	MAYBE	BETTER CHOICE
Big Bacon Classic	Garden Veggie Pita	Grilled Chicken
580 calories + 30 g fat	400 calories + 17 g fat	310 calories + 8 g fat
Chicken Caesar Fresh	Jr. Hamburger	Small Chile Stuffed Pitas
490 calories + 18 g fat	270 calories + 10 g fat	190 calories + 6 g fat

TACO BELL

DEADLY	MAYBE	BETTER CHOICE
Taco Salad with Salsa	Grilled Chicken Burrito	Tostada without Shell
850 calories + 52 g fat	410 calories + 15 g fat	300 calories + 15 g fat
Big Beef Burrito	Mexican Rice	Bean Burrito Supreme
520 calories + 23 g fat	190 calories + 9 g fat	380 calories + 12 g
Nachos Bell Grande		Pintos 'n' Cheese
770 calories + 39 g fat		190 calories + 9 g fat

CARL'S

DEADLY	MAYBE	BETTER CHOICE
Super Star Hamburger	Jr. Hamburger	Charbroiled BBQ Chicken Sandwich
Calories + 46 grams fat	330 calories +13 g fat	280 calories + 3 g fat

PIZZA HUT

DEADLY	MAYBE	BETTER CHOICE
Pepperoni Lover's Thin Pizza (2 slices)	Cheese Pizza (2 slices)	Veggie Lover's Pizza (2 slices)
770 calories + 32 g fat	406 calories + 20 g fat	380 calories + 16 g fat

ARBY'S

UNHEALTHY	MAYBE	BETTER CHOICE
Philly Beef'n Swiss	Giant Roast Beef	Light Roast Beef Deluxe
755 calories + 47 g fat	544 calories + 26 g fat	294 calories + 10 g fat
Deluxe Baker Potato	Italian Sub	Light Roast Turkey
736 calories + 36 g fat	671 calories + 39 g fat	260 calories 6 g fat

Reprint, "Guide to Your Child's Nutrition"

Problematic Salt (Sodium Chloride)

MOST AFRICAN AMERICANS CONSUME EXCESSIVE salt, and the youth are predisposed to their parents' or immediate caregivers' salt-eating habit. Ingesting more sodium than potassium creates a potassium deficiency in the diet—an imbalance of the two minerals, which may be linked to hypertension, fluid retention, strokes, kidney disease, or heart disease.

According to the American Heart Association, African Americans are afflicted with the highest rates of hypertension, death from stroke, and heart attacks in the world as a result of too much salt in their diets. For many African American parents and immediate caregivers, someone in their family has already paid the ultimate price—death. But an intervention must take place for the black community to become aware of the connection. Salt eating is a habit; it is an acquired taste that can be controlled.

The often fatal connection between salt, African American children, and predisposed ailments can be better understood by knowing how excess salt affects the human body. According to Barbara Dixon, RD, LDN (1994), table salt is 60 percent chloride and 40 percent sodium. Our bodies need a mineral found in salt called sodium to stabilize body fluids, control acid-alkaline balances, transmit nerve impulses, and contract muscles, including the heart. In addition, sodium eliminates carbon dioxide from the bloodstream and dissolves other blood minerals. As one can clearly understand, some sodium must be in the diet for optimal health.

Once the body is overloaded with sodium, it is programmed to expel excess sodium after normal usage. Safety devices located in the human body act as filters, sifting excess sodium through the kidneys and eventually expelling it through urine. If these safety devices were to malfunction, the kidneys would hold excess sodium. Consequently, the sodium attracts and retains water, which dilutes blood and makes blood volume rise. The more blood circulating through the body, the more the heart rate and blood pressure increase. Fluid retention can also cause blood clots, restrict activity, and cause mood swings. (Barbara Dixon, 1994).

Are African Americans Salt-Sensitive?

IT IS ESTIMATED THAT NEARLY 50 percent of people with hypertension are salt-sensitive. Physicians Russell and Suter (2001) maintain that there are many African Americans who are salt-sensitive, but no percentages can be rendered currently. What is salt sensitivity? It is the concept that makes people highly susceptible to any action salt may have on blood volume. Salt sensitivity is determined by reducing salt intake and measuring blood pressure to determine if the blood pressure is reduced. If the blood pressure doesn't fall with the reduction of salt, chances are there isn't sensitivity to salt. Although not all people are salt-sensitive, researchers have concluded that all those with hypertension appear to have a better chance of improving their health if they reduce their salt intake.

Potassium

SEVERAL YEARS AGO, MEDICAL RESEARCHERS conducted studies on the effects of potassium on the human body. They discovered how it relates to hypertension, which appears to be beneficial information for African Americans. "In the 1980s, researchers studying a group of hypertensives in Evans County, Georgia, found that hypertensive black adults consumed less potassium than whites with normal blood pressure, suggesting that increasing potassium may be especially helpful" (Dixon, 1994, p. 142). Equally important, potassium and how it relates to blood pressure can even impact those who have a hypertensive family history; that is, families with a history of hypertension can help counter this disease by lowering sodium and adding potassium to their diets to reduce blood pressure. The following is a list of high-sodium foods that can be detrimental to one's health as well as to unborn generations.

Table 2.4. Salt Sensations

Pizza	Soy sauce	Baking soda
Relishes	Table salt	Barbecue sauce
Salad dressing (dry and bottled)	Teriyaki sauce	Mayonnaise
Salted chips, nuts, popcorn, pretzels	Worcestershire sauce	MSG
Sausage	Pickles	Catsup

The influence of commercialism has led all Americans, including black Americans, to indulge in many of the items noted on the high-sodium list. Black children that believe the foods they consume are okay tend to repeat what they have learned and unconsciously self-impose all diseases associated with salty foods. Salt improves flavor, and people have become a nation obsessed with taste. Another flavor enhancer is MSG (monosodium glutamate), and the extent to which manufacturers will go to enhance taste is limitless. Regardless of the side effects of MSG, it's used in an enormous number of foods—chips, some Chinese food, and salad dressing. Foods that were once considered inexpensive and delicious should be viewed as a potential health hazard and not worth purchasing. The issue should be, what is a quality life worth?

Sugar

THE NEED FOR ENERGY IS essential in human development. We tend to garner energy from the sun. Likewise, we also consume energy, in the form of glucose, which is found in sugar. Sugars of all varieties contain glucose, which is the body's chief source of energy. Throughout the various stages of the African American's growth, from toddler through teen years, excessive amounts of sugar are consumed. Once the body utilizes the essential amount of glucose for proper bodily functions, the excess is stored as fat. As aforementioned in chapter 1, African American children view more television than any other ethnic minority. When children place themselves in front of a television, they snack, and more often than not, they snack on sugar-riddled nonhealthy foods.

Sugar is a crystalline substance found in the following foods: candy, juice, soda, jams, cookies, chocolate, crackers, hot and dry cereals, pies, ice cream, pizza, Jell-o, hot dogs, bacon, ham, salami, cold cuts, stuffing, breads, soups, mayonnaise, catsup, salad dressing, and fruit-flavored yogurt. Recent data by the American Dietetic Association (2001) reveal that Americans overall consume approximately 125 pounds of sugar per person annually. Parents and immediate caregivers need to read more food labels for the varied names for sugars—fructose, dextrose, lactose, levulose, and maltose. Basically, words ending in *ose* are usually synonymous with sugar.

The problem with refined white sugar is that it has been stripped of its mineral, vitamin, and fiber content. Natural sugars in fruits and vegetables afford sugar with fiber, which the body is able to process. In order to live healthy lives, African American children must be educated on how to satisfy their sweet tooth with nutritional sugars—plentiful fresh and dried fruits and limited low-in-sugar but high-in-fiber pastries.

Soda Pop

MORE FAMILIES HAVE INCLUDED SODA pop as a staple for social affairs. Oftentimes, when away from home, children will order a hamburger, fries, and a soda, which come in a variety of flavors: strawberry, cola, orange, grape, root beer, and clear-flavored. There were over fifteen billion gallons of soda pop sold in the United States in 2000 (*The Washington Post*, February 27, 2001,). Although this popular beverage may be enjoyed due to its taste, it's certainly not a nutritional refreshment. Hopefully, when black parents are educated about the deleterious effects of "liquid candy," they will afford a healthier alternative for themselves and children, such as 100 percent fruit juice—or even better, fresh fruit (fiber's included)—followed by water.

Black parents and immediate caregivers consider drinking sodas as an inexpensive choice for a refreshing drink. The cost of a soda ranges from thirty to seventy cents, whereas a bottle of fruit juice can cost almost triple that amount. According to author Michael F. Jacobson (2005), soda pop exacerbates tooth decay, bone weakening, obesity, heart disease, and kidney stones. The consumption of soda usually occurs at the dinner table, at restaurants, during family outings, at lunch, at work, at parties, while watching television, at school, and at the movies. There are many games played where soda is served as the primary refreshment—dominoes, chess, cards, and video games. It's a bad choice deeply ingrained in black culture's social events.

To prevent childhood obesity through good nutrition is to give a child an opportunity to live a healthy life and ultimately to contribute to changing African American culture for the better. Since the advent of slavery, the nutritional diets of African Americans have grown worse. At least during that period, fat from the hog was balanced with fish, wild game, vegetables, grains, and fruits. Today, poor eating habits are the result of cultural choices. In an age where information is abundant, African Americans are lagging in accessing it. The schools, the churches, and community organizations must pick up the slack. Hopefully, this generation will experience a higher health consciousness. See Appendix 1-A: Cultural Factors That Contribute to Childhood Obesity.

CHAPTER 3

———◄►———

Religion and the Contemporary Black Church

ALTHOUGH AFRICAN AMERICANS ARE MEMBERS of nearly all religious communities of the United States—Christian, Jewish, Islamic, Buddhist, humanist—most children are raised in Christian or Islamic homes. These two religions will serve as the focal point throughout this chapter.

Prior arriving in America, African Americans practiced religious traditions that were indigenous to African societies and were forbidden by the slave owners. Fear of an organized uprising and lack of respect for religions outside of their own version of Christianity were the plantation masters' motives. Africans, nonetheless, were successful at secretly practicing the religious beliefs they brought from Africa that were later infused with religious practices in this country.

There were many distinguishing factors of African religion prior to Christianity. Number one, they believed that one supreme God created the earth and all that is in it. Moreover, Africans believed that God was both male and female and had compassion for all things. Africans also believed that humans should treat each other with fairness, kindness, and respect. Other characteristics of traditional African religions were the holding of ancestors in high esteem. This is not to be confused with the worshiping of spirits of ancestors or the recently deceased as some have mistakenly thought. Traditional African religions placed a premium on collective and communal activities.

Since the introduction to European religions for Africans began during the early 1600s when they were transported to America via the slave trade, they were primarily exposed to Protestant Christianity. There were a few places in the British colonies that Catholics settled, and Catholicism was also introduced to Africans in America.

Author Larry Murphy (2000) explains that preachers and teachers from many different denominations worked among slave populations. This constituency included Anglicans (later called Episcopalians), the Society of Friends (also known as the Quakers), Congregationalists, Presbyterians, Catholics, Methodists, and Baptists. Africans, who would now be deemed as African Americans, were eventually drawn into the Christian faith through the range of churches sited above; however, most black Christians became Baptists and Methodists. Consequently, their original beliefs and religious orientation were altered by the doctrines and practices of their new faith (European-centered).

Also during this period of time, illiterate African Americans valued education, as they do today. However, originally, education was essential in order for deciphering literature they deemed sacred—the Bible. The impact the European version of Christianity had on African Americans is still apparent today. In many black churches it's evidenced by church walls and religious literature adorned with drawings and paintings of a white, blue-eyed version of Jesus, ironically representing a man from the Middle East.

History of Christianity within the African American Culture

AROUND THE EARLY SIXTEENTH CENTURY, Africans settled along the eastern shores of Jamestown, Virginia, and one of the first evidences of Christianity among Africans was noted when a Dutch military vessel sailed into a port at Jamestown, Virginia, offering to trade its cargo of twenty "Negroes" for provisions for the ship. Several of the twenty Africans who entered the colonies had European names. According to author Larry Murphy (2000), this was an indication that these Africans had undergone a Christian baptism, especially since at the time it was customary to assign all baptized individuals a Christian name. Per Murphy, there is evidence that suggests at least two of this group were united in marriage by a Christian church ceremony.

Initially, it was against white Christians' beliefs to own Christian slaves—until the mid-1600s, when church leaders and government policy makers abolished that rule. It was replaced by a new rule that stated anyone—that is, white males—could own a Christian slave. It not only became legal, but also acceptable, to the church for an African to be both a Christian and a slave.

Slave Converts

MOREOVER, DURING THIS TIME (MID-1600S), laypersons and individual clergy, along with some slave owners, sought to convert the rising colonial slave population to Christianity. Their justification was that they were bringing who they labeled heathers out of spiritual darkness into the light of the Christian faith; they were saving their souls from eternal damnation, which they perceived to be the fate of all nonbelievers. Throughout the 1700s, various Christian sects, including the Catholics in Maryland and Louisiana and the Methodist and Baptist churches, continued to impose a narrow, self-serving, imperialistic view of Christianity onto slaves.

In spite of efforts to convert slaves into Christianity, slave owners who stood to benefit from slavery objected to rendering religious instruction to African slaves. These objections are noted in the following concerns: "Would slaves who truly experienced freedom in Christ end up resenting and resisting human bondage? Would it make sense for masters and mistresses to become brothers and sisters in Christ?" (Murphy, 2003, p.20-21). Slave owners wrestled with the fact that if their slaves were given time for religious instruction, there would be a loss of productivity, and a decrease in profits would result.

In an attempt to address these issues, Christian teachings were revised. This conspiracy was to convince slaves that God advocated the slave system and the slave's Christian duty was to conform and be submissive. (This remnant of slavery still permeates the socialization of the African American child today; many parents explain their state of poverty and lack of opportunity as God's will, to which they must conform and submit.)

Furthermore, those who benefited from slavery never believed slaves should be converted to Christianity in the first place and did everything in their power to prevent their slaves from hearing and learning about Christianity.

In the nineteenth century, a paucity of preachers and religious teachers for both the black and white created a misunderstanding of the Christian message for slaves. The response of those who did hear the message was ambivalent. More specifically, enslaved blacks and free blacks were either rejecting or embracing the message. Many grew suspicious or resentful and held onto what they remembered of their native religion. Conversely, those slaves who did embrace Christianity did so to cushion slavery's cruelty and dehumanization.

Features of Christianity that the believers found attractive were as follows: God has a strong commitment to justice and freedom for the oppressed; God gave empowerment to the weak in the wake of brutality; and God has a heaven reserved for loyal Christians. This last feature provided the most hope.

The Enslaved and the Church

UNDER CHATTEL SLAVERY, AFRICANS HAD limited opportunities to worship as a result of being heavily scrutinized by slave owners. Slaves were not permitted to congregate in groups of more than two or three without a trusted white person being present.

Christian slaves, in turn, decided to gather in secret places for worship. Common meetings were in forest areas, by riversides, and in their cabins. Slaves had to be very creative and careful in the manner they worshipped. During this time, a slave caught worshipping was severely punished. According to former slaves, they had several methods to conceal sound so they could worship in safety. They would use wet blankets, speak low to the ground, and speak and sing into a pail of water. It is important to note that worshipping prior to 1863 was synonymous with survival and coping under nonhuman conditions.

Although the law forbade slaves to be taught to read and write, they were able to recite biblical scriptures—thus they memorized scriptures they heard in daytime services. For more detail, read Mechal Sobel's 1979

44

book, *Travlin' On: Slaves Journey to Afro-Baptist Faith*. At any rate, during religious meetings, slaves who could convince their audience that they were anointed for a divine calling were held in high esteem. Creditable attributes included knowledge of the Bible, evidence of piety, and oratorical skills (Murphy, 2003).

Christianity and Slave Resistance

AN ACT OF DEFIANCE BY Nat Turner, a Christian slave (1800–1831), intensified the fear slave owners held toward their slaves. At the age of twenty-five, he began having visions of liberating slaves on plantations. Turner claimed God gave him a sign to pursue his mission upon witnessing a solar eclipse in 1831 (Murphy, 2003). He led a revolt, August 22, 1831, massacring whites in different vicinities of South Hampton County, Virginia. It lasted two days. Eventually, they were overwhelmed by white police forces and hanged. Punishment resulted in seventeen hangings. Turner evaded police forces for approximately two months. Once Turner was caught, he was executed.

Approximately sixty whites were killed, triggering a pervasive fear across the South. Although this was not the first slave revolt, it was the most significant during this period. Turner's slave revolt heightened anxieties about Northerners who lived in the South, particularly blacks and those who were known as abolitionists.

On January 1, 1863, Abraham Lincoln signed the Emancipation Proclamation (a legal document that ensured all slaves in areas of rebellion against the United States would henceforth be free). During this time, two notable responses resulted from this legal document from a black Christian viewpoint. First, they rejoiced in what they believed was an act of God, rather than a political and economic strategy. January 1 was a day to be celebrated in the churches, giving praises to God.

Second, free blacks posed a serious threat to a system of racial slavery. The last thing the Southern white wanted was a black preacher to become more knowledgeable of the Bible, particularly texts on equality and liberty; however, emancipation set the stage for more literate black preachers. With missionaries from black denominations flooding to the South until the early twentieth century, a community of reverends emerged.

Unfortunately, the effect of emancipation was short-lived. During Reconstruction (1865–1877), civil authorities instituted black codes legislation, which was another method of reestablishing slavery. These laws restricted ex-slaves' movement; for example, they were required to make annual contracts for their labor, and if they ran away, they forfeited their wages for a year. More specifically, the black codes confined black interest and development. More can be read about black codes in Lerone Bennett, Jr.'s, *Before the Mayflower* (0000).

In 1910, a massive group of black Americans of the rural South migrated North, seeking economic opportunity. There were welcoming communities and Northern church members who helped accommodate the Southerners and integrated them into the new environment. In making this unprecedented exodus, the church as many Southerners knew it would never be the same. Southern Christians were accustomed to worshipping in small numbers, informally and in a lively manner. Once arriving at metropolitan places like Chicago, this was not the case; many Chicago pastors didn't sanction emotionally expressive worship. With this cultural shift made by Southern immigrants, they felt a lack of fulfillment and found it necessary to make adjustments.

The civil rights era was the next period in which religion impacted the lives of African Americans. Liberation was the central issue, as it was in the past. Liberation during the civil rights era embodied aspirations for legal protection and political rights. Prominent black Christian leaders that emerged from this era include Martin Luther King, Jr., Adam Clayton Powell, Fannie Lou Hamer, Andrew Young, and Joseph Lowery.

Black Muslims

THE HISTORY OF ISLAM DATES back to AD 632 with the flight of Mohammad; however, American black Muslims began in Newark, New Jersey, in 1913, with Noble Drew Ali, who established a Moorish Science Temple of America. His version of Islam was to help oppressed African Americans develop a sense of identity and pride. His followers were disillusioned with Christianity; it was labeled the religion of white Europeans and their descendents.

The movement was escalated by W.F. Muhammad after Noble Drew

Ali died in 1929. It's not clear if he came from Turkey or Iran, but Mecca was regarded as his birthplace. Like Ali, Fard Muhammad's teachings were designed to bring about black people's real identity as Muslims. He referred to his movement as "The Lost-Found Nation of Islam in the Wilderness of North America." The movement's leadership was eventually passed to a Georgia native, Elijah Muhammad, whom Fard Muhammad mentored. His doctrines included preaching separation from whites and regarding them as agents of Satan (the devil). Under Elijah's leadership arose Malcolm X, a national representative whose fame eventually overshadowed his own. Malcolm X became dissatisfied with the Nation of Islam and created a group that embraced more traditional principles of Islam. Shortly afterwards, Malcolm was assassinated.

After Elijah Muhammad's death, the Nation of Islam branched into two directions. Warith Deen Muhammad, Elijah's son and successor, headed one movement, and Louis Farrakhan, a charismatic orator who encouraged black Muslims to unify in resisting modern secular ills, headed the other movement. Both movements are currently active today.

When Islam Becomes the Religion of Choice

Many young black people are attracted to Islam, and there is no single reason. Some authors, such as Eric Lincoln (1990) and Lawrence Mamiya (1990), believe that Islam provides the long-deprived means of identification. For instance, the black Muslims helped forge Malcolm X's legacy of black nationalism. Malcolm X became an individual whom the youth could identify with and served as a hero to many African Americans, especially males. Moreover, black Muslims provide a clear-cut idea of a strong, macho, male image. More importantly, black folk, namely black men, are attracted to the black Muslims' stance against Western ideology (from European names to Western education). Lastly, Muslims spend a great deal of time in the prisons and on the streets—where the suffering is the most apparent—recruiting young black men and women into their faith. Most black Christian churches are not as active on this level.

The degree to which a religion addresses one's needs is an indicator of it becoming the religion of choice, and children who are raised in a religious community tend to remain in that religion as adults. However,

African American children who were once a part of the Christian faith, or who are of no religious persuasion and who have been incarcerated, are now confronted with a different set of needs and seek answers that appear to reside in Islam. This is particularly true for the young black male.

Christian Church for African American Children

AFRICAN AMERICAN CHILDREN WHO WERE faithfully raised in the Christian church become accustomed to worshipping practices that reflect the black experience. They observe their parents and immediate caregivers singing passionately from the depths of their souls. They become well acquainted with the Holy Ghost and the feeling of emotion that compels one to engage in a spirited dance or religious chant. To many, the hymns and gospels reflect the African American experience. Most black children don't understand the complexity of racial, social, political, and economic inequalities until their adolescent years, but they are cognizant of their family's and the church community's reactions to these societal ills.

In more recent times, the black church has made significant strides in meeting the social, financial, educational, health, and spiritual needs of the black community. Unfortunately, this phenomenon is not on a national level. Churches that currently operate under the evangelical tradition—a school of thought that suggests pastors convince their followers that they are "true servants of God"—set the stage for a religious culture that limits its services to a passionate sermon on Sundays and Wednesday's Bible study.

Traditional worship practices have played a pivotal role in turning African American families away from the black Christian church. According to Lincoln and Mamiya (1990), a Christian Methodist Episcopal (CME) pastor stated, "For the first time in black history, we are seeing an unchurched generation of young black people growing up in urban areas. In previous generations, you could always assume some knowledge of black church culture, like favorite hymns or prayers or some rituals. [Today] there are teenagers out there (in the streets) who have no knowledge of and no respect for the black church and its traditions" (p. 310). The group of unchurched black youth the reverend referred to are individuals born in northern and western urban areas around 1975 and

1980 (i.e., Generation X). This is not to suggest that the whole generation was unchurched, but a substantial number of this generation is of the unchurched population.

There are a few reasons that African American children are unchurched. As mentioned previously, at times in the community the reverend's evangelical philosophy has become obsolete and irrelevant; the church has failed to meet the needs of the community. During the 1970s and 1980s, many churches failed to make shaping racial identity a priority among black children. Drawings and paintings of biblical characters and biblical materials were devoid of black representation. However, the majority of black clergy of black Methodist denominations (AME, AME Zion, and CME) indeed used Sunday school literature with black representation. Most black churches also fall short in providing quality educational programs—that is, an education that both maximizes intellectual capability and includes cultural representation.

Black reverends that lived by the evangelist philosophy usually lacked the formal training that was so desperately needed in the black community. Many found themselves in a situation where the supply of educated ministers was in far less abundance than the black communities' demand. Lincoln and Mamiya (1990) maintain that their "survey and field experiences indicate quite clearly that the most creative and innovative forms of ministry in black communities today are being carried out by the better educated clergy at the large urban black churches" (p. 399). Better-educated clergy have and will continue to reverse the unchurched effect. Unlike in the past, today's ministers have the capacity to address a whole spectrum of human needs.

The Progressive Black Church

TOO MANY AFRICAN AMERICAN CHILDREN are born without the knowledge of their culture. The birth of a child should create enthusiasm for parents and caregivers to shape or mold specific beliefs, attitudes, and values. They should acquire them not only from the home, but also from the school, community, and especially the church.

Today's progressive black church is stepping up to the plate—they are surpassing traditional church services. Many churches, particularly in southern regions of the United States, are now addressing the crises of young African American males in the criminal justice system. It is reported that in some urban areas, as many as a third of black males between the ages of seventeen and twenty-one are under the jurisdiction of the criminal justice system (Billingsley, 1999).

Ministers in the religious community have found that many of the problems of early encounters with the criminal justice system were interrelated with problems at school. In response, ministers in the religious community are now organizing schools to meet the needs of troubled black male youth. When one minister was questioned for reaching out to the urban community, his response was, "This is the purpose of the progressive black church—to meet the needs of the black community" (Billingsley, 1999). Currently, one of the most pressing needs is to assist black youth to successfully complete high school. These faith-based organizations draw upon different strategies—in addition to religious teachings—to address this problem. These males are provided adult supervision, assistance with homework, tutoring, recreation, and training in African American history as well as biblical history.

Some of the more common problems African American youth (particularly males) wrestle with in public schools include learning styles, behavioral difficulties, and interracial settings (see chapter 1, title). Due to a breakdown of family and community, many African American youth today also experience feelings of hopelessness and demand immediate gratification, which breeds gangster mentalities by both male and female. Indeed, these conditions breed trouble and detachment from humanity, which manifest in killing, raping, and honoring distorted value systems. According to Noam Chomsky, renowned professor (1994, p. 39), "Grim circumstances without much prospect for a future or for constructive social action, express themselves in violence." The success of these church schools is dictated by reverends networking with several organizations, which include, but are not limited to, the following: local police departments, judges, junior high and high school administrations, and juvenile courts.

Unlike the public school system, the progressive black church holds each student accountable for individual and group success. Highly driven tutors and mentors work with at-risk African American males in less chaotic learning environments. Their troubled lifestyles have been intervened in by these school systems, which have created the format for these young people to turn their lives around—to succeed in high school and beyond.

Many scenarios can send the youth pummeling down trouble lane. Public school teachers usually reduce aggressive behaviors from black males to pathology. Thus it is imperative for African American children to be educated in a climate where they are understood and valued.

The success of faith-based alternative schools has been proved. Teachers in these settings have exceptional giftedness, strong commitment, patience, and creativity. Results of the church-based initiatives build character in once hopeless students, using strong religious devotion, moral development, and academic principles. Today, the progressive black church operates upon a new set of standards to produce better students—better human beings.

Middle-Class Blacks at White Churches

SINCE THE 1964 CIVIL RIGHTS Act, the black middle class has risen to new heights in social and economic status. This bill created a vast middle class by allowing them to acquire those careers and employment that they were originally excluded from. This upward mobility was instrumental in setting the stage for a unique psychology among middle-class black Americans. This thought can be better understood by reading works by Calvin Marshall in Marvin A. McMickles *Preaching to the Black Middle Class* (2000). Marshall maintains that the not-so-new phenomenon with black middle-class people leaving black churches for white churches is the work of the "Afro-Saxon mind." He contends that in America and the Caribbean, the Afro-Saxon mentality is a dynamic concept in which middle-class African Americans rank themselves among other members of their group membership by virtue of their economic status. In fact, according to William Turner, director of black church affairs at Duke University Divinity School at Durham, North Carolina (Perryman, 2003), "Many of the black churches have changed and now define success out of American corporate reality. That definition includes: fancy cars, itinerant executives, and corporate careers, like many white churches" (p. 30). Distinct symptoms that are typical of this trend to assimilate include fleeing the black ghetto and moving into integrated neighborhoods, and acquiring membership in interracial churches, country clubs, and yacht clubs. These individuals are determined to attain every success level or symbol of affluence of the dominant culture. Often the adults as well as their children suffer alienation from their heritage and cultural identity.

Middle-class African American children who attend predominately white churches are indirectly taught that issues affecting their blackness in America are not significant. Placing minimal emphasis on blacks' contributions to society inadvertently teaches the child that black people's contributions are insignificant; subsequently, the child learns to define his own existence as insignificant.

Black pastors around the country are concerned that social and political issues that affect them will always take a backseat in the predominately white church. Marvin A. McMickle, author of *Preaching to the Black Middle Class* (2000), urges black people in the white church and white preachers to think about the following questions: Are white churches capable of assisting their black youth to grow up with a positive sense of self-identity and self-esteem? Will white churches be willing to invest a percentage of their resources into black-owned banks or credit unions? Will the white church be willing to meet the needs of the black community with projects such as black-owned small businesses, insurance, or other black interests? Overall, many black pastors are struggling with middle-class blacks who attend predominantly white churches to consider the following: are these faith-based institutions moving toward shaping a just society?

Spirituality

THE WORD *SPIRITUALITY* IS COMMONLY mistaken for religion. Today's African American youth are in need of a belief system that empowers them, gives them direction, and forces them to individually develop a fundamental knowledge of themselves. Today, it is understood that self-identity and a sense of direction usually go hand-in-hand. In most cases, those without a belief system—in God or any other higher power—become involved in destructive tendencies or behaviors. It is apparent that some form of spiritual connection is necessary. So, where does spirituality fit into this picture?

A definition is in order and can be complex—some will maintain that it's a complex phenomenon. According to Richard Wolman, author of *Thinking with Your Soul: Intelligence and Why It Matters* (2001), spirituality is "to acknowledge the specific religious or ritualistic aspects of spirituality, items that pertain to prayer and meditation were included. Spirituality may be thought of as encompassing religion or religiosity, because it is clearly a broader and more comprehensive phenomenon than the latter. Spirituality also pertains to a person's attitude and stance toward the outside world, the world of social organization, and to the view he or she has of past, present, and future" (p. 128). Similarly, Saint Teresa and Maharshi maintain that spirituality is from within, the result of recognition, realization, and reverence (Dyer, 2001).

This author believes that spirituality is too abstract to be defined. Spirituality sets itself apart from organized religion in that one does not need to meet at the church or mosque to express their faith. Moreover, individuals who practice spirituality can tailor it to accommodate each personal need. Spirituality is particularly important to those African American parents and caregivers who are dissatisfied with organized religion and some of its questionable principles. It's all about how the individual chooses to think rather than perpetuating a practice endorsed by their parents or caregivers or religious leaders.

Living in the twenty-first century as an unprepared and unequipped African American is problematic. Given the grim criminal justice statistics of the African American male and female, along with the fact that there is a massive decline of young African American males in the church (both Christian and Islamic), should serve as a wake-up call that organized religion, no matter how progressive it has become, is not the sole answer to the challenges met by the youth.

Ministers of different faiths will either declare the devil has control of young African American spirits, that secular culture is the problem, or evade the issues. Distinguished colleagues in academia are likely to attribute the problem to a combination of conspiracies and social ills. And parents and immediate caregivers tend to respond by saying, "He or she just won't do right," "I can't get them to listen," or "Nothing I do seems to work." The point is that African American children have been failed somewhere down the line in their socialization process.

Before our youth can progress in a world that is becoming increasingly interdependent, public schools will have to be reformed. The religious community will have to be redefined, and the black church's meaning and purpose will have to be instilled in African American children, and at an early stage, before a crisis occurs. Seeking a sense of spirituality for guidance, solace, and purpose is difficult with the market-driven culture's conflicting messages selling materialism.

Black Theology

PASTORS FROM THE CONTEMPORARY BLACK church have evolved into a theology that places blacks as central reference points. Critics have labeled this school of thought as black supremacy—a vehicle that causes racial divisiveness. Yet reverends, parents, and immediate caregivers embrace this theology because it is the result of the struggle oppressed people faced in America, a struggle which initially attracted blacks to Christianity. The theology offers hope. However, the pitfalls of black theology are that its scope can be narrow, and like any other religion, it is rife with sexism.

Sexism in the Contemporary Black Church

ONE OF THE GREATEST IRONIES in religion is sexism. Regardless of the progress of Christianity, particularly in the African American community, sexism exists with authority. Ironically, the Bible speaks of fairness to all people, yet the behavior of black religious leaders reflects an omission of this holy principle. African American children who attend Sunday school listen to ministers whose messages exclude women from religious text. It has a dynamic effect on the youth—as sophisticated as they are, they are influenced by sexist attitudes, spoken and unspoken. It essentially becomes a part of their psyche, consequently creating another generation of young people opposing aspiring women.

It is also apparent that there is a decline of black males in the rural church communities. In one study conducted by the distinguished author Jawanza Kunjufu (1997), in which he interviewed 75 African American men, it revealed twenty-one reasons that they didn't attend church. Interestingly enough, many of Kunjufu's findings suggest that it was during many of the participants' childhoods and adolescent years that problems emerged. Barriers that contributed to African American men turning away from the church are as follows:

1. Hypocrisy
2. Ego/dictatorial
3. Faith-submission-trust forgiveness-angry at God
4. Passivity
5. Tithing
6. Irrelevance
7. Eurocentric
8. Length of service
9. Too emotional
10. Sports
11. Attire/dress code
12. Classism/unemployment
13. Education
14. Sexuality and drugs
15. Homosexuality
16. Spirituality/worshipping/ alone universalism
17. Heaven
18. Evangelism
19. Lack of Christian role models
20. Streets/peer pressure
21. Parental double standards forced when a child

In recent times, African American parents and immediate caregivers have been fighting an uphill battle for children in a culture that undermines basic human values—tolerance, unconditional love, service to community, delayed gratification, and religious and spiritual devotion. At the center is how well each parent and immediate caregiver grasps fundamental methods of raising religious and/or spiritually connected children in America.

The assumption of most African American Christian households is that if children are raised in a religious environment, they will adhere to religious principles, such as the Ten Commandments; respect for their parents, elders, and themselves; and thinking twice before succumbing to destructive habits. This notion is, in part, held due to the countless hours parents and immediate caregivers invest in their offspring. The parents and caregivers who raise their children in Christianity reinforce their expectations with sermons, gospel music, religious texts, and other religious media. Moreover, youth ministries and Sunday school can serve as a positive influence in troubled black children's lives. Therefore, African

American parents' and immediate caregivers' expectations of their offspring are based on exposure to a religious persuasion and model of spirituality, which can be a good determinant for a bright future.

African American religion began in 1619 with slaves' arrival to Jamestown, Virginia.

However, African American religion has evolved out of necessity to meet the needs of the community. Listed below is a timeline that depicts those changes.

African American Religion Time Line

1619   A Dutch ship arrives at Jamestown, Virginia, trading twenty Africans for food; it marks the introduction of slavery into what became the United States.

1787   Black worshippers at the St. George Methodist Episcopal Church, Philadelphia, walk out as a result of racially discriminatory treatment.

1794   The Saint Thomas Protestant Episcopal Church is founded in Philadelphia.

1816   Bethel Church, Philadelphia, joins with other black Methodists to form the Independent African Methodist Episcopal Church.

1821   The African Methodist Episcopal Zion Church is organized.

1831   Nat Turner, an enslaved Baptist preacher, leads one of the most extensive slave revolts, causing the virtual shutdown of missions to the South.

1863   Emancipation and the conclusion of the Civil War (in 1865) open up the South to mission work by black denominations, which mushroom in size.

1870   The Colored (later Christian) Methodist Episcopal Church is formed.

1875   James Augustine Healy is made the first African American Catholic bishop.

1895   The National Baptist Convention, USA, Inc., eventually to become the largest black denomination, is formed by the merger of three groups.

1897   The Church of God in Christ is incorporated.

1900   Migration of African Americans from the rural South begins to pick up. From 1900 to 1930, some two million blacks make the move to north and west.

1906   William Seymour leads the Azuza Street Revival, out of which developed the Pentecostal movement.

1930   Wallace D. Fard Muhammad begins the preaching in Detroit that launches the Nation of Islam.

1963   Baptist minister Martin Luther King, Jr., leads a march on Washington, where he delivers his celebrated "I Have a Dream" speech.

1964   Malcolm X breaks with the Nation of Islam and forms the Muslim Mosque, Inc., and the Organization of Afro-American Unity.

1978   Warith Deen Muhammad, son of Elijah Muhammad, moves the Nation of Islam into the larger family of worldwide orthodox Islam, changing his organization's name to the Muslim American Society.

2000   Rev. Vashti Murphy McKenzie is elected bishop in the African Methodist Episcopal Church, the first female bishop in a historically black denomination.

Source: *Spiritual Perspectives on Globalization: Making Sense Of Economic And Cultural Upheaval. Ira Rifkin (2004).*

The philosophical debate over the significance the church and religion play in the lives of African American children is a topic that will be debated throughout time. Some feel that the black churches are not addressing the needs of African American children in the twenty-first century and that many males bypass the black church altogether because they believe answers they're seeking must be found in other places.

African Americans possess a history of coping with inhumane hardships in which they found relief by adopting a Christian faith and later the Islamic faith. Today, African American youth who have no religious affiliation need spiritual food in order to navigate through unprecedented social pressures: body piercing, drugs, sex, violence, gangs, cyber crimes, online dating, and other irresponsible and destructive behaviors. Culturally conscious adults should consider organizing professional associations that would bridge the gap between the churched and unchurched youth and provide the spiritual tools needed to assist them to cope, adapt, and develop strong and sound minds during their development process in America. Although community organizations should participate in this movement, the black church has the capacity to spearhead this reform. They have the finances, a pool of talented educators, and the desire to create relevant ministries.

CHAPTER 4

— ◄ —

Politics

CURRENTLY IN THE AFRICAN AMERICAN community, not much emphasis is placed on garnering a fundamental political education. Most African American children are indoctrinated to blindly register and vote as Democrats and under their tutelage aspire for economic and social opportunities—good jobs, decent housing. In effect, without knowledge of self-determination and the need to control the economics of their community, African American children are unconsciously prepped to despise their own community and love someone else's—namely, white folk and others who are collectively organized.

Those in power achieve this flagrant status via propaganda, bribery, money, and deceit. One theory holds that by influencing minority group thinking, more can be controlled, and most importantly, more minorities are unlikely to pose a threat to the ruling class. With the exception of a few, many black politicians of today are no more effective now than they were in the era of historian and educator Carter G. Woodson (1875–1950). He maintained that once blacks are appointed to high-ranking government offices, they conveniently forget about relevant concerns affecting the black community. Those that are in mainstream organizations frequently exchange small kickbacks that only benefit them for supporting certain candidates for office. Issues such as economics, education, police brutality, the disintegration of the family, high incarceration rates, and drug usage are ignored. Carter Woodson stated that "These Negro workers are supposed to tell their people how one politician seeking office has appointed more

Negro messengers or chairwomen in the service than the other or how the grandfather of the candidate stood with Lincoln and Grant through their ordeal and thus brought the race into its own" (1990, p. 92). This classic strategy was implemented again during the Clinton administration by employing more African Americans to high-ranking positions in his administration than any other president in U.S. history. There were four who occupied seats in the president's cabinet: Ron Brown, Mike Espy, Jesse Brown, and Hazel O'Leary.

Another classic technique that politicians use on black Americans is pitting one party against the other, usually the Democrats against the Republicans. Historically, neither party has effectively addressed black folk's needs as a people. Yet blacks tend to vote blindly and in an uninformed way for both Democrats and Republicans. Regardless of the perceptions of Republicans and Democrats, both parties have historically demonstrated loyalties to special interest groups and corporations.

Doing for self or even supporting those who are self-employed is too much to swallow for some African American parents and immediate caregivers. Instead, they relentlessly advocate relying on government handouts as a way of life, creating a never-ending cycle of generations of African American youth who accept and perpetuate this existence.

As mentioned previously, the extent of the black community's political affiliation is primarily based on assimilating into white politics with little or no control. With the exception of a few grassroots organizations in various communities, black youth witness and mimic these acts of assimilation.

Most African American Democrats tend to become collectively sensitive to anyone challenging their affiliation. Republicans are routinely perceived as overtly racist, against providing any government benefits, and refusing to distribute handouts to poor people, which includes a large proportion of blacks. Political awareness in the African American community is, at best, something in between voting Democrat and staying as far away from a Republican's agenda as possible.

Very few African American parents and immediate caregivers understand how politics actually works in America. The bulk of their knowledge is extracted from television, which is intertwined with propaganda. Whatever African American parents' perceptions or philosophy are, they usually influence their offspring with them—the youth's first initiation to political awareness.

African American children are introduced to the Pledge of Allegiance on the first day of kindergarten. This is the beginning of their institutional-political experience. That's followed by class officers' elections, which usually occur in the third or fourth grade. This is significant for those who are curious about elected officials in the real world. School elections are a positive introduction to politics. Each child will respond differently; some will be motivated to pursue further political activities or knowledge, and others will disregard politics entirely, but all will be affected. Unfortunately, not enough African American parents nurture this interest in the election process, because they don't know how, or they're unconcerned, or they feel their children will learn about the election processes when they're older.

Historically, role models were a factor in the child's political orientation. Observing black female or male politicians effecting change encourages African American youth to aspire to leadership roles, regardless of attitudes learned at home. Today African American youth and youth of color around the world can find a role model in American's first African American president—Barack Obama. Unlike past political administrations, President Obama is making government more accessible, relevant, and engaging to people in America, which will have a lasting impact on African American children and youth in the future. This was in part accomplished by utilizing technology of the 21st century such as cell phones, social networks (e.g., Twitter, MySpace, FaceBook), text messages, and the Internet.

There are not enough parents who are familiar with current legislation that affects the community. African American parents and immediate caregivers who do not place a premium on constitutional rights and civic duties and responsibilities , inadvertently render the issues insignificant or futile. From parents who choose not to vote or feel their vote is futile, the youth conclude that black people have no political power.

Occasionally, African Americans will become involved in organized uprisings about a perceived injustice, such as the 1990s Rodney King beating or the 2000s George W. Bush presidential election, in which all votes weren't counted. Indeed, more African American adults, as well as their children, will be driven into desperate channels due to political indifference or ignorance. Whether or not this pressing problem can be resolved is dependent upon a resurgence of a political consciousness throughout the black community.

Elders in the black community, particularly those from the Depression era and the baby boom generation, tend to view voting as a necessary right. Their outlook or worldview was and is shaped by two significant historical events: The Great Depression (1929–1940) and the civil rights era (1955-1968). Common factors that these two pivotal events share can be summed up in one word—struggle. Individuals from the latter generation can recall picket lines, countless protest marches, numerous walkouts, water hoses, and attack dogs.

One of the goals of the civil rights movement involved gaining the right to vote, which triggered the voter registration movement— registering the youth as well as the elderly. This generation acquired information, history, and wisdom from the Depression era generation, but little or no information was passed down to Generation X (those born approximately1966–1977). Unlike the baby boom generation, who suffered political strife, Generation X and their children, Generation Y (those born approximately 1978–1998), appear to lack knowledge of voting duty or urgency that's necessary to change the socioeconomic climate of the black community.

Avoiding Past Mistakes

UNLIKE PREVIOUS GENERATIONS, GENERATION X is the first to be raised free of legalized segregation, not experiencing great blacks such as Martin Luther King, Jr., as a political hero; most importantly, they live in a society that aggressively promotes an ideology of free market enterprise. The African American youth who lack these fundamental experiences have little chance of avoiding the mistakes of their forefathers. This is not to suggest that all hope is lost with Generations X and Y. There are some within these generations who are endeavoring to make a difference. There are members in the hip-hop community who are setting an example by using politics as a vehicle to benefit the poor and oppressed people of color. These efforts are courageous and bold; they're positioning black youth to determine the correct path at the crossroads of materialism and liberation.

History of Democrats Appeal to African Americans

ON A COLLECTIVE LEVEL, LIBERALS have manipulated black leadership throughout the past century. Organizations such as the old National Association for the Advancement of Colored People (NAACP) were conditioned to sit idly by awaiting legislation that guaranteed handouts to the black community.

A common theme in history is that people, particularly those in positions of leadership, typically have an agenda that is the driving force behind their actions. In this instance, the Democratic Party will be the focal point. Prior to the period 1866 to 1928, the African American vote was unanimously for the Republican Party, but the African American attraction to the party waned, primarily due to the party's lack of full concern for civil rights. During this period, the black press, such as the *Pittsburgh Courier* and *Norfolk Journal*, were growing increasingly critical of the Republican Party. Another contributing factor for the movement to the Democratic Party was frustration from a weak economy, for which the Republicans were held responsible.

Some historians suggest that the switch of African Americans' political affiliation from Republican to Democrat was not clear-cut. John Hope Franklin echoed this in the following statement: "The break was neither clean nor complete, however, for there were those who could not be persuaded to support the party that, after all, was the party of the Ku Klux Klan and other bigots" (Perryman,2003, p. 36).

Blacks had always experienced hard times since their forced migration to America. The Depression did not impact African Americans as it did Anglo-Americans. Instead, it was black newspapers—the means of mass communication and propaganda—that convinced the black community that the Republican Party took the black vote for granted.

Democrats, in turn, packaged old wine in a new bottle, and it worked. African Americans figured that the Democratic Party would be the more attractive alternative. Twenty years later, after blacks had acquired voting rights, demographic segregation was still prevailing. Requests for a permanent civil rights commission were denied, and the African American standard of living had not improved. African American newspapers began losing their voices of authority and were replaced by the injustices preached by black ministers. This eventually set the stage for the civil rights movement of the 1950s and 1960s.

Democratic politicians knew what appealed to the younger civil rights generation and began promising to address issues affecting African Americans: racial injustices, poverty, and employment discrimination. In addition, candidates from the Democratic Party promised to pass legislation that would address pressing issues in the African American community in exchange for their votes. Author Wayne Perryman notes, "While many younger blacks were willing to give the Democrats their votes, some of the older blacks who knew their history were reluctant and skeptical" (Perryman, 2004, p. 47). The older generation, or Depression era generation, personally experienced racial injustices in the thirties and forties with Presidents Roosevelt and Truman. Acts of specific injustice toward blacks are cited in Wayne Perryman's *Unfounded Loyalty* (2003). Clearly, acts of violence were apparent with the Democratic Party during 1870–1930. To seize control of the black vote, during the 1960s, Democrats ratified the 1964 Civil Rights Act, which was welcomed, but inadvertently undermined grassroots and other self-help efforts within the black community.

An effective movement to politicize black youth must begin with the history of struggle. It should be taught in the home, in the church, and in other organizations throughout the community.

CHAPTER 5

———▸ ◂———

Self-Esteem

SELF-ESTEEM CAN BE DEFINED AS the individual's personal judgment of his or her own self-worth: the sense of personal worth associated with one's self-concept (Atwater, 1996). Without a doubt, the parents and primary caregivers of African American children will influence their children's self-worth; however, other contributing factors are the conflicting external forces—the values set by their peers, the media, or society in general.

Throughout African American children's developmental process, they receive positive reinforcement or negative consequences for their actions. When television becomes the substitute for parenting, as it has in many African American homes, the esteem of the children is at risk. As early as three years old, they learn to despise everything about themselves—their hair, eye color, skin tone, facial features, and body structures—because they don't look like the people they primarily view. More specifically, parents and caregivers must realize if they're not already cognizant of this issue, that they are dealing with the larger-than-life media images. In a recent article, Victoria Ward, EdD, a professor at Simmons College and author of *The Skin We're In* (2000), stated, "When black children look in the mirror, they see that there is a total mismatch between the image staring back at them and the one that the media has embraced" (April 2002, *Essence*, p. 124). At their very worst, parents and immediate caregivers can expect their child to reject everything associated with blackness and become subjected to rejection from white people in an attempt to assimilate. Thus the African American child will be marginalized upon becoming an adult if immediate action is not taken.

This condition is most difficult to avert, primarily due to an inadequate support system that is much needed while the child is in a fluctuating state of self-love and self-hate. Nonetheless, parents and caregivers are not totally powerless in the self-esteem-building battle. Useful tactics of affirmation are necessary.

For females, an early affirmation of her natural beauty and her abilities is pertinent. Also, toys, books, and videos that reinforce black beauty and applaud female accomplishments prove helpful. For the males, it is also pertinent that he is exposed to toys, books, and videos that applaud male accomplishments. Culturally specific achievements should be especially introduced in the home, because they are suppressed in mainstream society. Most educational institutions fail to extol African Americans' achievements. Others recognize black Americans' contributions solely during Black History Month, failing to understand that black youth need reinforcement 365 days per year.

There is no one answer for this problem, but some negative influences are more problematic than others. Obviously, parents are the most influential figures in a child's life. For the most part, siblings are the next influential, then friends, teachers, religious leaders, coaches, and other community people.

A child's confidence is usually something that should be nurtured by parents as well as educators, friends, and other people of the community. It is the mother, normally the first teacher, who usually initiates the process. Ideally, "the formula" for esteem building should be utilized by all who are in the child's life: the bonding, providing the child opportunities, encouraging the child to set and accomplish goals, accepting the child as a unique human being, and instilling cultural identification.

Circumstances that contribute to the countering of this socialization process are the devaluation of African American people, as well as of other people of color, and ignorance of African/African American history and its place in the world's vantage point. Many parents are totally oblivious of themselves and of their history and are frustrated by racism that affects their livelihoods. Others have thriving careers, but are blinded by their longing to be accepted and praised by people of a higher rank within the dominant culture. Both situations are setbacks for feeling worthy, which trickle down to the children. Parents who feel bad about themselves are unable to nurture positive feelings in their children. Any environmental situation void of good formula ingredients delays or denigrates the child's esteem-building processes.

A twenty-four-hour support system is another aspect of building confidence in children. They need to spend adequate time at home under parental or caregiver guidance. Of course, there are circumstances when this can't happen. Parents' careers, working two jobs, or attending school prevent them from being there. And the youth who are in search of filling this void often resort to joining a group of peers who appear to have "the formula"—gangs. Although the black youth's attraction to gangs is undesirable, gangs manage to meet their every need. The bottom line is the need to belong to a group—the need for a family will be satisfied either at home or on the streets.

Gangs only serve as the barometer or as a reflection of someone or something that has failed African American youth. Many gang members and experts who research and write about them maintain that this population is about belonging or identity. Aside from the direction that the street gangs are headed, they replace voids that parents and the community should address.

Experts suggest that the average black home has television programs running almost eleven hours per day. During this time, a multitude of sexual images permeates the youth's subconscious. Black youth, particularly black females, suffer from negative media images. There have always been negative images and stereotypical behaviors portrayed in many classic as well as contemporary Hollywood movies, such as those featuring the Jezebels and welfare queens. Light-skinned, well-toned, half-naked, thin black women epitomize the perfect woman in rap videos. Young girls react with either a common sensibility or with a feeling of resentment for what they view as ideal.

Negative rap images that are affecting African American females are largely due to corporate America's devaluation of black women. Experts suggest white youth are the consumers of 70 percent of rap music sold world-wide, therefore corporate America constructs images and verbal content that appeals to their target audience. All too often, many of the rap videos depict young black women as objects of male's sexual conquest. Moreover, rap lyrics frequently allude to black females as hoes and bitches. The negative labeling of black females in turn get internalized (usually unconsciously) by those who listen to rap music which becomes destructive to black females self-esteem.

Some of the insidious psychological impacts that sexually charged images create are the onset of premature adult behavior in black adolescents. They are choosing irresponsible sexual relations, and the girls become pregnant and their childhoods are compromised. Ultimately, they are thrust into an adult role before they are ready to assume the responsibility this requires.

Today's entertainment market is aggressively prostituting hip-hop culture. Its influence can be seen in almost every industrial culture worldwide. However, the threatening impact it has on mainstream America serves as an affirmation that African American youth must understand how they are perceived by people outside their culture. Dr. Richard Majors, a psychologist at the University of Wisconsin–Eau Claire, has committed years to studying and advancing the understanding of black masculine self-expressions, such as demeanor, speech, gesture, clothing, hairstyle, walk, stance, and handshake (Goleman, 1992). Living in a society in which African American youth are devalued, alienated, and made to feel inferior, their expressions can be perceived as antisocial, when they are actually attempts to express their feelings—their self-worth and need for recognition. Wearing expensive sneakers, jewelry (or imitations), clothing, and braids are manifestations of their feelings and their connection to each other.

Hair Matters

FROM THE TIME AFRICANS ARRIVED on American soil, their folklore, history, and culture have been distorted, suppressed, falsified, and ultimately crystallized into self-hate. Knowledge of one's correct history sets the stage for the direction a people should pursue to advance their role in creating a better world. African Americans have been flagrantly written out of world history, creating a sizable cultural void.

Western or European curriculum is rooted in the notion that being white is basically enviable and desirable, and too many African American females deem white female images as the standard of femininity. Hair color, style, length, and texture become critical issues in their self-image-building process.

Author Ingrid Banks ascertains that African American women share a collective consciousness about hair. Most of them consent to similar motives for altering hair texture. Many learn at an early age that in order to obtain the attention of a male, they must look as close to that which is the epitome of femininity—white females—as possible. However, the average black female feels that straightening her hair, which also lengthens it, has nothing to do with her image of herself; they feel it's easier to maintain and is acceptable by the white and black employers; it's considered as being professionally presentable. Research confirms these notions. After interviewing several African American women regarding their hair, author Ingrid Banks had one interviewee that stated, "You are considered much more feminine and much more alluring if your hair is long. The longer your hair is, the more feminine you are" (Banks, 2000, p. 41). No doubt, this is the justification for hair extensions, weaves, and wigs.

Without question, African American women are dealing with a cultural and political construction that stems from mainstream notions of beauty. Furthermore, these females are also conditioned to believe that they are more feminine "being able to toss [their] tresses back in grand sweeping motion, and from side to side" (Banks, 2000, p. 42). This is a task that only real women can do with a straight style. Nevertheless, as Banks suggested, there is great social and cultural significance of black hair/ hairstyling practices and black females' identity. During the Marcus Garvey movement, African Americans were urged to assert their indigenous culture by wearing their hair natural. Slogans such as "Black is beautiful" were also typical of the era.

Making reference to good and bad hair should cease, because it is often taken as a literal truth—straighter hair is considered good and nappy hair is considered bad. Children and some adults lack the proper perspective for understanding the philosophical debate of good and bad hair. We are all children of God, and God "don't" make no ugly or bad hair. Black musical artist India Arie wrestles with hair politics in her song,

"I Am Not My Hair." this song can heard on the Testimony: Vol. 1, Life & Relationship album.

Eating Disorders

A FEW AFRICAN AMERICAN GIRLS have stopped eating properly as a direct result of pop culture extolling thinness. Today very few females escape the domination of the mass media programming. Entertainers who once represented the average body type have now conformed to mainstream ideal body image. The psychology behind this particular attitude and behavior is that African American females decide they must emulate the entertainers to be desired and loved. However, the extent to which African American girls are willing to identify and conform to attain this ideal body image is alarming. More middle-class black females are developing a surge of eating disorders. More than 90 percent of those who suffer from eating disorders are adolescents and young adults, according to the National Mental Health Information Center (2002).

Culturally speaking, African American females who are more susceptible to eating disorders (mostly eating too little or purging) are the following: young, overweight, well educated, identify with white women, and uphold middle-class values. Historically, eating disorders were perceived as something that white women experience; at least, that was the prevailing assumption, although current research suggests that any ethnic group is susceptible to an eating disorder given certain circumstances.

Treatments employed include interpersonal psychotherapy, which is a method used to help people examine their relationships with friends and family, then to make changes in problem areas. The next method is cognitive-behavioral therapy, which teaches patients the techniques to monitor and change their eating habits as well as to alter their coping mechanisms. Another useful method is medication such as antidepressants. The key is to seek professional help.

Warning Signs for Eating Disorders

- [ ] Abnormal weight loss of 25 percent or more with no known medical illness accounting for the loss
- [ ] Intense fear of gaining weight
- [ ] Peculiar patterns of handling food
- [ ] Amenorrhea (an absence of the menses) in women
- [ ] Exhibition of bulimic episodes of binge-eating followed by vomiting and/or laxative and diuretic abuse

Some Physical Problems Associated with Eating Disorders

- [ ] Cessation of menstruation
- [ ] Chronic kidney problems
- [ ] Irregular heart rhythms
- [ ] Irritation and tears in the esophagus
- [ ] Parotid gland swelling (under jawline)
- [ ] Erosion of tooth enamel and increased cavities
- [ ] Electrolyte imbalance
- [ ] Low potassium
- [ ] Lightheadedness and dizziness or fainting

Building Self-Worth

INDEED, DURING THE SOCIALIZATION PROCESS, the African American child's circumstances and obstacles can and often do damage their sense of self-worth. Those children who are raised in a verbally or physically abusive environment often carry those wounds into adolescence and adulthood. They will lack adequate coping skills when making the transition from elementary school to junior high and then on to high school.

Many cannot measure up to the pressures of ideal beauty images: physical attractiveness, slimness, and fashion trends for females, and height, tight/muscular body, and fashion trends for males. However, each individual's self-worth fluctuates in different facets of his or her life.

African American youth, along with other ethnic minorities, spend seven to eight hours in classrooms bombarded with white images as masters of creations and productions. As discussed in a previous chapter, systematically excluding African American youth from contributions to world civilizations and history suggests that their people are worthless and, even worse, invisible.

Limited ethnic representation in the public school systems' curriculum is the root of the problem that most ethnic groups encounter in America. Obviously, an entire school system cannot become reformed overnight, but more multicultural dialogue needs to take place amongst parents, concerned citizens, teachers, education board members, and business leaders. A discussion of ethnic curriculum infusion is essentially a discussion about providing an atmosphere in which the students are able to feel good about their individual culture. This is just the first step. Introducing a multicultural curriculum into the public school system would ideally serve as a balance for all ethnicities to be recognized as contributors to world civilization and history.

Martial arts instructor Ron Boswell of the ATA Black Belt Academy, maintain that they are successful at increasing self-confidence in children via praise. In fact, "the biggest thing with Attention Deficit Disorder ADD and Attention Deficit-Hyperactivity Disorder (ADHD) kids is to praise them on little things to build their confidence," Boswell said. "Once they have confidence, they can do anything (Gang, 2004)." Equally important, most instructors agree that African American children who learn self-defense training or martial arts learn discipline. The principles of the discipline can be used in all aspects of African American children's endeavors.

Black children should be exposed to extracurricular activities, such as debate teams, chess clubs, bands, drama clubs, choirs, sports, Business Professionals of America, and other organizations that build character. In many cases, this selection of extracurricular activities is not available to students in most rural and a few inner-city schools. Moreover, some

African American youth find praise and reward in traditional sports such as baseball and basketball. No matter which extracurricular activity the youth select, it eventually contributes to their sense of achievement.

Participating in extracurricular activities teaches the youth communication, teamwork, and strategy planning skills. Extracurricular activities, such as a band, club sports, and the chess club are essential to the African American child's development, especially character development. For example, "acting in plays can teach students to make decisions under stress, because no matter how much they rehearse, it's inevitable that something will go wrong during a performance, and the students will have to handle it on their own (Wells, 2009)." Far too often, black youth are placed in school situations that stifle character development. Furthermore, participation in extracurricular activities is a desirable quality that many colleges value; it enhances the youth's chances for admission.

Skin Matters

If you're white, you're right

If you're yellow, you're mellow

If you're brown, stick around

If you're black, get back

Way back!

ELAINE BROWN, A COMMUNITY ACTIVIST, like countless other African American women, recalls the rhyme of skin privilege in the black community. This statement reinforces favoritism and privilege that has existed for years. However, the historical significance of skin privilege appears to have originated in the antebellum South on slave plantations. Wilson and Russell claim that slave owners accepted what is called the mulatto hypothesis: "That an infusion of white blood would lift Negroes out of their base of inferiority, as a result, they began selecting lighter-skinned female slaves, some of whom were their own offspring, for the high-status household jobs of nanny, cook, and seamstress" (Flowers, Garrett, McMillan, & Robert, 2006, p. 79). Slave owners reserved field duties such as plowing, planting, and harvesting to the darker-skinned slaves. The rationale behind this was that blacks of darker hue were better able to endure the sun's intensity.

According to Bell Hooks, color-caste hierarchies were represented in everyday life and media. "Without a doubt dark-skinned black females suffer the most abuse when black people internalize white-supremacist notions of beauty (Hooks, 2005, p. 70)." Equally important, the notion of equating light-skinned women with desirability and social status tends to have a less negative impact on African American females self-esteem. "A fair-skinned black female who may be able to feel that she is lovely and desirable because of her skin color may rely so much on looks to negotiate her way through daily life that she will not develop other areas of her life, like a grounded personality or her intellectual skills (Hooks, 2005, p. 69)." African American women who have been socialized within Western European institutions learn and act upon the subtle bias, which is passed on to their children.

The Strong Black Woman Concept

THROUGHOUT THE YEARS, BLACK WOMEN developed a set of personal beliefs that was influenced by their socialization process. Somewhere between birth and womanhood, the black woman's self-esteem was tainted, which can be reversed. Developing and maintaining a healthy sense of worthiness results from two practices. First, black women must tell themselves that they are lovable. Second, black women need to tell themselves that they are worthwhile (Boyd, 1993, p. 5).

A phenomenon that occurs with black women is equating womanhood with the amount of duties that they assume. This strong black woman concept may have its origin in slavery. Black women who perpetuate this behavior, particularly single black women, may be setting up themselves and their daughters up for disappointment. Author Julia A. Boyd maintains, "When we can't live up to everybody's idea or expectation of a strong black woman, we feel like a failure, and feeling like a failure only leads to big-time depression" (Boyd, 1993, p. 15). This is an indication that black women often risk their sanity in an attempt to fulfill this image. Moreover, mass media perpetuate stereotypes of what a strong black woman should be. Hollywood recognizes the strength of actress Angela Bassett, actress/

dancer Phylicia Rashad, and career-driven individuals such as producer/businesswoman Oprah Winfrey. More importantly, these subtle messages are passed to young African American females, and if they fail to measure up to standards and if they aren't armored with acceptance and praises by their parents or caregivers, they're more likely to succumb to the programming of unworthiness.

The Shifting Concept

Two AUTHORS, CHARISSE JONES AND Kumea Shorter-Gooden (2003), coined a term, *shifting*, which involves a black person (normally a female) altering one's outward behavior, appearance, attitude, or voice tone from one moment to the next in the presence of white folk, and one of the pitfalls of shifting is that it hinders one from living an authentic life. However, as most minorities realize, shifting (as discussed by Jones and Shorter-Gooden) is employed as a tactic of survival in an unjust, antihuman, masculine-driven, and racist society. In the presence of African American parents or immediate caregivers engaging in shifting, black children model what they see and what they hear.

Actually, shifting could be a useful tactic to instill in African American children as a facet of their socialization. Ultimately, it may become a necessity in African American children's pre-adult and adult lives; for example, shifting may well be needed for a child or adolescent in a predominately white school. Black children who are provided with a model of standard English usage, a respectful attitude, and a socially acceptable appearance would fare much better than the black child who upholds to opposite examples. Again, this is about survival in a hostile society.

Awareness of shifting strategies is equally important in relationships and in social situations. African American girls need to know from adult examples that their capabilities, ambitions, and achievements need not be scaled down in an attempt to secure the interest of a man. From their first role model, their mother, and from other female role models, they need to know that it is okay to be smart, lovable, and desirable.

The same holds true in the African American church, where several testimonies were written by several black women in the book *Shifting:*

The Double Lives of Black Women in America (Gooden & Jones, 2003). For starters, the black church is plagued with sexism. Black women are the backbone of the church, and yet they are often subjected to male chauvinism, justified by slanted interpretations of biblical scriptures. No African American female or male child should have to be reduced to a mindless submissive pawn or second-class citizen at a house of worship, where everyone is ideally equal in the higher power's eyes.

Self-Victimization

SOME PSYCHOLOGICAL THEORIES MAINTAIN THAT behavior is learned. "Children learn not only through classical and operant conditioning but also by observing and imitating others" (Evans, 1989). While growing up in African American culture, children as young as five and six years old master reverse racism and self-victimization and suffer their effects. Some of the most common themes of self-victimization in the black community are, "The black man can not succeed in the white man's world." Or, "I can't find a decent job (with or without my degree); it must be racism." Most black children are bombarded with these attitudes throughout their adolescent years. A study was made of a sixth-grade public school class in Montgomery County, Maryland, and the results were featured in a *Washington Post* article entitled, "Stereotype Within." Twenty-four out of twenty-nine black students believed they were inferior (Elrich, 1994). The article suggested that the children felt their inferiority was innate. In fact, several prevailing misconceptions the black children held were noted in *The Washington Post* as follows:

- Blacks are poor and stay poor because they are dumber than whites and Asians.

- Black kids who do their schoolwork and behave must want to be white. White kids who do poorly or dress cool want to be black. Hispanic kids want to be black because they aren't smart like whites.

- Black people don't like to work hard.

- Blacks don't need to work hard because it won't matter in the end.

- Black people have to be bad so they can fight and defend themselves from other blacks.

- Black men make women pregnant and leave.

- Black boys expect to die young and have money.

- White people are smart and have money.

- Asians are smart and make money.

- Asians don't like blacks or Hispanics.

- Hispanics are more like blacks than whites. They can't be white, so they try to be black.

At the root of African American children's plight with negative messages and stereotypes is America's white supremacist culture. African American children internalize these misconceptions largely due to their parents and caregivers. In spite of popular belief, racists, politicians, teachers, rappers, comedians, and other entertainers are not fully to blame. On the contrary, it's the parents' and caregivers' primary responsibility to actively shape the thought processes of their offspring. To suggest that someone else is at fault for actions of one's own is an act of denial—self-inflicted victimization. Blaming others not only intensifies the problem, but it also provides children and their parent's excuses for failing to assume responsibility and accountability.

Again, by playing the victim role, black people have no motive to be responsible. Many African American parents will watch television shows during their spare time instead of seeking African American history and achievements information to share with their children. Consequently, parents and immediate caregivers, not knowing anything about their past, unconsciously will their children a contract of self-victimization and inferiority. Above all, where there is no expectation, accountability, or standards, the self-victimization and inferiority complex will be molded, internalized, and self-maintained.

Parents or immediate caregivers need to seek the correctives by sifting through these destructive messages and beliefs, and then critiquing them and presenting the truth to their children. A family could begin with weekly round-table discussions of African Americans' contributions or achievements or struggles at home and abroad.

Stages of Black Racial Identity Development

FOR SOME BLACK YOUTH, RACIAL identity is acquired abruptly. Circumstances are the key factor. Youth who grow up in an environment absent of nonblack people may experience a black identity development later when they are forced to interact with members of the dominant culture (whites). However, two eminent African American psychologists Janet Helms, and William Cross, have created models of ethnic identity development that will serve as a reference point in explaining the African American child's self-concept in America and worldwide (Atwater, 1996). There are four stages of identity development:

Stage 1. Pre-encounter

The pre-encounter stage is marked by African American youth playing down the significance of race in America. Some at this stage even deny race is an issue at all. Their contention is that people are judged on their character rather than race. According to Beverly Tatum, a black person in this stage has "absorbed many of the beliefs that white is right and black is wrong" (Tatum, 1992, p. 331). More importantly, the poet Paul Lawrence Dunbar explains it all too well in his "We Wear the Mask" poem.

> We wear the mask that grins and lies,
>
> It hides our cheeks and shades our eyes,
>
> This debt we pay to human guile;
>
> With torn and bleeding hearts we smile,
>
> And mouth with myriad subtleties.
>
> Why should the world be over-wise,
>
> In counting all our tears and sighs?
>
> Nay, let them only see us, while
>
> We wear the mask.
>
> We smile, but, O great Christ, our cries
>
> To thee from tortured souls arise.
>
> We sing, but oh the clay is vile

Beneath our feet, and long the mile;

But let the world dream otherwise,

We wear the mask!

Stage 2. Encounter

The encounter stage is marked by an incident in which an African American youth is forced to become aware of his or her race. It is very common for African American youth to experience racial profiling or be subjected to overt racial slurs.

Highly acculturated middle-class youth often become very confused at this point because they cannot understand how someone of the dominant culture can reduce them to a *nigger* while they do everything in their power to uphold white middle-class values. Another example of the encounter stage is when an African American youth is on a prom date and borrows the family car, a BMW, only to be stopped by a white police officer for suspicion of an alleged robbery. As one can imagine, encounters, as such, can be overwhelming.

Stage 3. Immersion-Emersion

In the immersion-emersion stage, African American youth become more curious about their culture and tend to place a premium on the values of their indigenous culture and disregard values of the dominant culture. It is not unusual to see African American youth also develop Afro-centric tendencies at this stage. For instance, they will go to great lengths to prove that everything significant stems from black people. How emotionally scarred the individual is will determine the duration of this pro-black stance.

Stage 4. Internalization-Commitment

Finally, moving into stage four requires African American youth to balance their pro-black attitudes with the dominant group's culture. Beliefs and values outside of their own are respected. They no longer alienate themselves with members of the same race. The scope of their once narrow worldview is broadened.

Developmental Growth

AUTHOR COURTLAND C. LEE (1996) highlights several additional phases of developmental tasks that can potentially become problematic during the socialization process of African American children and youth (namely, males). Racism, coupled with a slave mentality, is at the root of many youth and adults who are emotionally, cognitively, and socially stifled. African American parents who aren't equipped with correctives fail the youth. They lack the basis for understanding the reality of why so many African American males/females are not developing to their potential. One of the modern-day symptoms of inadequate psychological development is youth and adults living in the now rather than making the most of today with plans for the future. They fail to grasp the need for planning their future. In addition, an unprecedented sense of self-worthlessness plays into this mind-set. Below is an outline of childhood/adolescence (youth) psychological development.

Childhood

- Recognize self and others based on color

- Incorporate racial labels into evolving self-concept

- Recognize, identify, and label social inconsistencies; e.g. racism, discrimination, prejudice

- Recognize and develop skills for negotiating multiracial environments and bicultural experiences, each containing mixed and contradictory messages

- Forge an appropriate and healthy identity in the face of racism, discrimination, prejudice

- Fine-tune sensing and judging skills to screen out or transform negative racial/color images and messages

Adolescence

- Refine a healthy identity which transforms and/or transcends societal messages of inferiority, pathology, and deviance based on color, race, and/or culture

- Strengthen skills for negotiating bicultural and multicultural environments

In addition to most African American parents and immediate caregivers, today's public school systems are not equipped to deliver such race-specific developmental skills. Consequently, both African American males and females will continue to feel inadequate, which affects their emotional and social growth, academic achievement, and career development throughout their lives unless parents or caregivers abort this epidemic.

Rites of Passage

SEVERAL EDUCATORS BELIEVE THAT RITES-OF-PASSAGE programs are needed in the African American community, particularly when high incarceration rates exist among our youth.

A rites-of-passage program ensures a developmental and transformational process, often culturally specific, whereby adolescent girls and boys undergo a set of rituals that prepare them for adulthood. For example, a Baltimore Rites-of-Passage Program implements the following components:

- Arrange African traditions or influences at the core
- Involve parents, relatives, and guardians in the process
- Make the rites-of-passage program an ongoing process
- Give the participants tasks to master
- Include rituals and ceremonial activities in lifestyle
- Allow the community to witness the ceremonies

Another issue must be examined to understand how critical rites-of-passage are in the holistic development of the African American child. Whether the programs are formal or informal, they must be strong enough to deter the youth from seeking affirmation from gangs or by pregnancies. Effective rites-of-passage programs serve the youth's inherent needs for self-esteem, acceptance, belonging, and racial identity.

Therefore, if rites-of-passage regimes are implemented on a pervasive level, mentally healthy youth will prevail, and fewer generations will be at the mercy of the U.S. government's diminishing social assistance programs, the streets, and the criminal justice system.

Self-esteem is an important aspect of the emotional, intellectual, and spiritual development of African Americans. All children should feel good about themselves in order to persevere through life's obstacles and challenges, particularly in the twenty-first century. Without this sense of worthiness, youth tend to travel down the road of poor school performance, bad relationships, inability to sustain a job, incarceration, death, and drug or alcohol abuse.

CHAPTER 6

— ➤ ◄ —

The Biracial Child

THE NOTION OF RACE AND culture as we know it in America has shed light on several pitfalls of white superiority. Biracial children do not fit into the narrow scope and confining paradigm of black and white, minority and majority. America's white supremacy thesis fails to include race outside the black/white dichotomy box; consequently, most biracial children, especially those black and white, experience identity crises, alienation, confusion, and heartache while being socialized throughout their childhood and pre-adult years.

Biracial individuals can be best defined as individuals who are biologically or culturally from two or more races, ethnicities, or cultures, such as black-Latino or white-Asian. The scope of this chapter will primarily address issues that the black-white biracial children undergo into their post-adolescent years.

Challenges Encountered by Biracial Individuals

BIRACIAL YOUTH, PARTICULARLY ADOLESCENTS, TEND to wrestle with identity development more so than non-biracial youth. The greatest portion of this struggle is finding a safe place to celebrate both heritages. A child of both white and black ancestry needs a safe place within the family in order to socialize with both the white and black communities.

In an attempt to find a safe place to exist and to develop their identity, the youngsters are essentially forced to choose either blacks or whites.

Racial politics in America suggests that a biracial child—namely, one with African American blood—is automatically black, regardless of phenotypical traits. Four- or five-year-olds experience racial politics firsthand, according to Tatum (1997). The following scenario is of a biracial child experiencing a challenge to his identity:

Sam is a six-year-old child. His mother is white and his father is black. Sam's father always dreamed of his son playing football. So he signed Sam up for a neighborhood-sponsored team. Several games had passed, until one day, one of Sam's teammates called him a white boy, due to his fair skin. Although this situation escalated into a physical fight amongst Sam and his peers, it confused him because he viewed himself as black.

Similar incidences occur to biracial children in white circles. It is not uncommon for biracial children to live in predominately white neighborhoods. In fact, many biracial children recall living in white communities and being taught to devalue their black selves and culture (Brown, 2001).

According to author Sundee T. Frazier (2002), identity begins with acceptance of self. For a person to solely rely on other people's image or definition of herself or himself results in confusion. In a study done by Barbara Tizard and Ann Phoenix (1993), they interviewed a biracial adolescent child who suggested that the most common factor that contributes to biracial youth identity is racism and its ramifications. Furthermore, they interviewed an adolescent biracial child who expressed the following regarding racial identity: "At first, I only included Afro-Caribbeans or Africans, but now I realize [black] is a word that's more ambiguous than your color or your features or anything. It includes an attitude of white people towards black people towards themselves ... As far as the white person is concerned, black is 'other' ... they'll see someone other than white coming down the street, so that's what made me realize I'm black" (Tizard and Phoenix (1993). As confused as most biracial youth are about their identity, situational and individual racism nearly forces them to side or identify with either the black or white race. Nonetheless, this is not to suggest that they refuse to celebrate both cultural heritages; many embrace both.

The struggle for identity becomes evermore complex when biracial youth cannot separate acts of institutional racism from their white heritage. As some have expressed, it's hard to identify and find comfort with white people, because of the plight of the black community. Racist comments, particularly within the adolescent years, become more obvious because of peer groups, cliques, and conformity.

When job seeking or filling out questionnaires, biracial youth who are in limbo about their identity have to decide which race to claim: Caucasian, black, Native American, Asian, Hispanic, or other. The youth and some adults who don't have a clear sense of identity typically check "other." The rationale is that they feel they're a product of two cultures, not one; therefore, selecting "other" is the closest thing to recognizing his or her mixed heritage.

International biracial children, who are socialized outside America, tend to view and identify their mixed blood with the indigenous country or continent from which their parents originated. A British and African (living in Britain) child would not regard himself as black; instead, he would identify himself as British African. Therefore, he is able, most of the time, to distinguish himself from racial politics, unlike his American counterparts.

In many cases, parents' thoughts on mixed heritage tend to be positive and healthy. Most parents tenaciously urge their children to embrace both heritages. Parents and immediate caregivers draw upon terminology such as "half and half," mixed race, or mixed ethnic group when describing their child or when engaging in dialogue with them. Above all, these parents feel and teach their children pride of being a product of mixed ancestry.

Interracial parents rendered the following statements about mixed parentage: "I think I made it clear [to the children's father] that I would not have them brought up as either black or white, because that was unfair on either one. If you bring them up to think they are black, they lose out on the white side, and vice versa. You can have the best of both worlds, and I was determined I would give it to them … They have been brought up to be very proud of what they are, and proud of their color, and proud of how lucky they are to have two countries" (Tizard and Phoenix, 1993, p. 151). Conversely, some interracial couples find a need to downplay one race over another with their children, as in the following statement: "We don't have discussions in terms of her being a mixed race, we discuss her in relation to her being black, because that's how she sees herself" (Phoenix and Tizard, 1993, p. 150).

Identity Fluctuations

IN DEVELOPING A RACIAL IDENTITY, biracial or mixed-race people are faced with their own unique set of challenges—namely, deciding with which group to identify. Ursula M. Brown, author of *The Interracial Experience (Growing Up Black/White Racially Mixed in the United States)* (2001), conducted a study that suggests biracial identity tends to solidify at a later age than non-mixed-race people. (See Table 6-1.)

Table 6-1.
Racial Identity during Various Developmental Periods

Race	Black (%)	White (%)	Interracial (%)	Other (%)	Not Sure (%)
Ime					
Preschool	16.8	14.3	19.3	2.5	47.1
Grade school	25.2	21.8	33.6	3.4	16.0
High school	29.4	10.9	54.6	5.0	
After high school	29.4	4.2	57.1	9.2	

(Rows add to 100% (except where due to a rounding error.)

Mixed-race youth often report feelings of inadequacy, partly due to inadequate feelings of close friends or associates. One youth reported that her first cousin felt that she was secretly denying a part of herself, her white heritage, because in public she prided herself on being black. According to Ursula Brown, psychotherapist Joel Crohn interviewed several black/white students in a group setting, he found a similar phenomenon. "Eight out of the ten students identified themselves exclusively as black in the group setting, but in one-to-one interviews, results changed to the opposite. Eight out of ten said they identified mostly as interracial" (Brown, p. 47).

Apparently, a mixed-race child and youth's identity is subject to fluctuation from one group to the other.

History of Mixed-Race People in America

THE HISTORY OF MIXED-RACE OR biracial people in America has always been turbulent and marked with ignorance. Since the mid-1930s, social scientists have relied on nonempirical evidence to clarify their understanding of mixed-race people. There were several prominent theories held in reverence during that time. However, the hybrid degeneracy theory is most noteworthy.

The "hybrid degeneracy" theory emerged near the end of the Civil War and lingered until the mid-1930s. It maintained that interracial people "were supposedly emotionally unstable and biologically inferior to both their racially homogenous black and white parents" (Brown, 2001, p.37). American sociologist Edward Reuter was quoted as stating, "The mixed blood is [by definition] an unadjusted person" (Reuter, 2007, p. 216). Charles Benedict Davenport maintains, "One often sees in mulattos an ambition and push combined with intellectual inadequacy which makes the unhappy hybrid dissatisfied with his lot and a nuisance to others" (Brown, 2001, p.37).

Their "unnatural blend" supposedly made mulattos depressed, moody, irrational, discontented, impulsive, confused, nervous, etc. Moreover, mulattoes (i.e., mixed-race people) were depicted as "criminal, sterile, not harmoniously proportioned in body, more prone to tuberculosis and to child birthing difficulties" than whites or blacks (Brown, 2001).

However, most oversimplified generalizations maintained by people of European descent were premised on several racist notions.

"First, the mulatto inherits the vices of both races and none of the virtues; second, any achievement of a Negro is to be attributed to the white blood in his vein. The logic runs that even inheriting the worst from whites is sufficient for achievement in Negroes. The mulatto is a victim of divided inheritance; from his white blood come his intellectual strivings, his unwillingness to be a slave; from his Negro blood come his baser emotional urges, his indolence, his savagery"(Brown, 2001, p. 194). However, this is not the first historical perspective of a so-called mulatto.

In fact, there are several variations of mulattoes. Noted below are the various types of mulattos that entail the biracial experience.

Variations on a Theme of a Mulatto

Standard Mulatto: This type of mulatto includes having a white mother and black father.

African American: The most common form of mulatto in North America; this breed is not often described as mixed, but is nevertheless a combination of African, European, and Native American. Moreover this mulatto may come in any skin tone, and of any cultural background.

Jewlatto: The second most prevalent form of mulatto in the North American continent is the Jewlatto mulatto. This breed is made in the commingling of Jews and blacks who met while registering voters in the South during Freedom Summer or at a CORE meeting. Jewlattos will often, though not necessarily, have a white father and a black mother, and more likely to be raised in a diverse setting, around others of his or her kind, such as New York City (Greenwich Village) or northern California (Berkeley).

Mestizo: The Mestizo mulatto is a more complicated mixture, where either the black or white parent claims a third race in their background; for example, Native American or Latino, which confuses the child more. The mestizo is likely to be mistaken for some other, totally distinct ethnicity, such as Italian, Arab, Mexican, Jewish, East Indian, Native American, Puerto Rican.

Gelatto: The Gelatto mulatto is a combination of Italian American and African American, this breed often lives in either a strictly Italian neighborhood if the father is white (Bensonhurst) or in a black neighborhood if the father is black (Flatbush). Usually, the child identifies strongly with one side of the family over the other.

Source: Half and Half: Writers on Growing Up Biracial and Bicultural, Claudine C. O'Hearn

These misguided doctrines continue to cause the most damage by being systematically institutionalized and unchallenged. The effects of these theories have caused many divisions among whites, blacks, Asians, and Native Americans, by virtue of skin color, class, hair, and physical traits, just to name a few. Often the parents of mixed-race children stereotype their children, inadvertently perpetuating myths and half-truths: All blacks can dance or sing or when you're white, you're right. Until this incorrect information is contested, it will continue to be passed from one generation to another.

At any rate, racist, misguided theories did not shift until the black power movement in the 1960s. This is not to suggest that previous ideologies were dismissed during this time. Instead, this was a point at which a new ideology challenged an old ideology.

Upon racial identity formation for biracial youth a vast, complex amount of information is taken in primarily from their immediate environment. The key to developing a positive identity is for their parents and/or immediate caregiver to expose their children to other positive biracial youth and adults. Developing a healthy self-concept will ultimately take time and much parental involvement, particularly in shaping their political/social identity. Listed below are social and political factors that help to shape biracial identity.

Factors Related to Biracial Identity Formation

- Identity formation in general usually begins in teenage years and lasts until early into the mid-twenties.

- Racial, ethnic, cultural identification is a core part of self-identity.

- Physical factors such as skin color, physique, facial, and hair features influence racial identification.

- A biracial youth's social status may influence his or her desire to be a part of a group (racial) membership.

- Exposure to cultural customs increases knowledge of and identification with a group.

- Biracial youth who have positive relationships with both parents tend to form positive mixed race identities.

- Racial awareness may develop more slowly in some biracial children due to their limited cognitive capacity.

- Biracial youth who have access to a multiracial peer group find the support they need to form positive self-identies.

- Biracial youth prefer the label "biracial or multiracial," included from the U.S. Census Bureau.

- Biracial youth needs biracial role models for confusing questions and support.

Although forming a biracial identity can be a confusing time for the youth, there are some social and political realities that can shape their identity.

Social/Political Reality Shapes Biracial Identity

- Biracial individuals may internalize conflicts between groups.

- Groups of nearly equal status allow for greater social and economic mobility—e.g., Asians and Americans—increasing the likelihood of acceptance from both.

- White supremacy and institutionalized racism may inhibit biracial identity development.

- The reality of group oppression is a unique consideration for African descendants.

- Personal identity needs should be balanced within a political context.

Independent of celebrating both cultures, children of black and white parents should be prepared for society to regard them as black. Regardless of who they are on the inside, America's one-drop rule unfortunately exists. More often than not, society will judge them accordingly, particularly those who possess strong African American facial features. According to behavioral theorists such as Jean Piaget (2001), biracial children as young as seven and eight have a limited cognitive capacity. Piaget maintains that complex reasoning such as understanding racism does not occur until the "period of formal operations, which is from age eleven or twelve and up in years." Therefore, coping mechanisms should be presented in an age-appropriate manner.

Which Parent Should Prepare a Biracial Child for Racism?

SOCIAL ILLS MANIFEST THEMSELVES IN many forms; regardless of the type, ideally children are in general need of some level of orientation. Children of mixed-race should be taught about racism by their parent(s) or immediate caregiver as early as grade school. Race, for instance, in America still matters (West, 1994). As a result of racism, which significantly affects the African American community, methods must be conjured up for coping. Blues, jazz, rap, rhythm & blues, and Afro-centricity are some of the creative outlets that we've created as a result of our painful suffering (West, 1994). Nevertheless, parents and immediate caregivers should seriously consider a black or another person of nonmajority status to instruct their offspring on how to survive and deal with racism. Ursula Brown notes that "the black parent may be more adept in preparing a child to cope with racial bigotry. Never having gone through life as a person of color, the white parent may not react to racism the way a black person does" (Brown, 2001, p. 112). As a result, he or she may not be as sensitive to essential coping skills and ultimately do more harm than good. This is not to suggest that white parents have nothing valuable to add to the dialogue about racism. Biracial children need to hear how both parents feel about racism, but usually one parent is more effective in preparing the child for societal attitudes.

The biracial experience is more immediate or blatant than that of African Americans of same-race ancestry. The child has parents from two distinct races, requiring the youth to constantly juggle his or her identity—the youth is constantly shifting.

A mixed community is optimal for socialization of biracial children, according to author Ursula Brown, 2001; consequently, the children are exposed to a group of people who affirm each other's differences and similarities. If raising children in a mixed community isn't an option, perhaps organizations that include a sizable number of mixed-race children could be sought. After all, underneath the external confusion are young humans needing to relate to others like themselves, yearning to be validated. It is basic human nature to gravitate to and identify with individuals who reflect a similar image.

CHAPTER 7

—▶ ◀—

Sex Education and Sexual Abuse

THIS SOCIETY AS WE KNOW it has become more and more obsessed with sex and sexual content. Sex dominates in all modes of mass media because sex sells, and it has engulfed the youth. However, today's concerned parenting figures must eventually engage in a conversation with their children on sex and sexuality.

Sex is defined as the act of two consenting individuals (preteens and teenagers included) engaging in sexual intercourse. This is an activity in which the involvement of youth is phenomenal. Unlike past generations, more African American youth (Generation Y) are engaging in sex at a younger age. As a result, it is imperative that parents and immediate caregivers begin discussing this subject matter early, rather than prolonging it until adolescence or post-adolescence. To an extent, past generations, especially those prior to the Depression era, had reservations about openly discussing sex with their children: they felt discussing it encouraged participation, plus it was simply taboo; consequently, a substantial number of baby boomers did not receive sex education from their parents.

Baby boomers were the generation to really develop liberal sexual attitudes, which in turn were passed down to Generation X, evolving into irresponsible sexual behavior, but this generation can be rescued. Their irresponsible behaviors can be reversed by initiating an aggressive sex education program in the schools and dialogue in the homes. Thus, future conversations between parents and children will become less anxiety-ridden, which would be an immediate result.

During adolescence, many physical changes occur in males, such as the growth spurt, lowering of the voice, and hormones kicking in. This stage of adolescence serves as an indicator to both parents and immediate caregivers that a talk about the responsibilities and consequences of sex is due. Whoever possesses the most influence in the male's life will be most influential with the sex talk. In fact, according to authors Nancy and A.J. Franklin, "From research we know that many fathers and close male role models will influence adolescent boys to be more sexually active, as compared to a mother's influence" (Franklin and Franklin, 2000, p. 142). This attitude must cease and sex education programs for parents as well as their children must be implemented.

During and even prior to adolescence, African American males receive inaccurate information regarding relationships and sex with females. The parents and immediate caregivers are handicapped (for the most part) in providing the proper framework for clarifying fact from fiction, lie from truth, and propaganda from complex reality. This is primarily due to their parents being mis-educated, which perpetuates a cycle of confusion.

When African American youth buy into what appears en vogue from peers and mass media, it's a chore to teach them different behavior. The root of this pressing problem is within the African American community: the perpetuation of slave mentalities—folks thinking they own each other and making irresponsible sexual demands of each other. It's up to each parent and caregiver to assist in reversing this process.

Are Black Women Hypersexual?

DURING SLAVERY, BLACK WOMEN'S BODIES were often treated as property and objects of desire. They were scantily clothed and were frequently stripped, especially for whippings. White men came to associate naked black female bodies with sensuality and promiscuity, particularly when compared to white women, whom were placed on a pedestal as the epitome of beauty. Stereotypes emerged regarding black women being available for sex anytime and anywhere with anybody, even for a fee.

African American parents and immediate caregivers who strive to raise so-called "good girls"—studious, well-mannered, ambitious, and nonpromiscuous—must wage a war against stereotypes. They're propagated by many institutions, especially the mass media, which often contradict positive messages taught at home, church, and in character-building schools.

The Sexual Revolution

BEYOND A SHADOW OF A doubt, it is apparent that America has become less safe for children, and the sexual revolution could be partly blamed. In the sixties, women declared that they were free to have as many sexual relationships and perform the same jobs as men. Today, it encompasses the usage of sex to sell commercial products, such as liquor, automobiles, and even foods. However, according to author Sol Gordon, a sexual revolution is "a new morality whose main ethic is everyone should be free from repression and should do his or her own thing, or, simply, if it feels good, do it" (Gordon, 2000, p. 2). Couple this with TV ads promoting instant gratification, and a whole generation of African American youth are inoculated with distortions and misinformation about sex. More specifically, Dr. Paul C. Reisser (1993) maintains that four main fantasies are depicted by the sexual revolution. They are as follows:

1. Sex is okay any which way, and with whomever, as long as there is mutual consent, no one gets pregnant (unless she wants to), and no one gets hurt.
2. Sex is usual and customary if you are attracted to someone.
3. Sex unrelated to marriage is normal, natural, expected, and inevitable, so carry a condom.
4. If you are postponing sex until marriage, you must be incredibly unattractive, a social disaster, or a religious fanatic.

As aforementioned in chapter 5, African American children view more television than any other ethnic minority group. If they are not isolated, and are frequently exposed to sexually charged material that sanctions impulsive sexual desires, licentious vantages, and surrendering to sex initiation, parents, teachers, and immediate caregivers can expect serious consequences. Unbridled passion and unprotected sex result in teenage pregnancy and less education, coping skills, and resources. Living in a culture that serves sexual temptation on a silver platter creates even more difficulty for African American parents. These folks are finding it necessary to teach their offspring about sex as young as five or six years of age; the younger the child, the less information is required, but details should be tailored to their emotional maturity level.

There was a time prior to the sexual revolution when, if at all, the sex talk came closer to the onset of a girl's menstruation and a boy's nocturnal emission. Prior to the 1990s, more television shows promoted family solidarity and delayed sexual encounters. That's all changed now. America's current market-driven culture serves as a wake-up call that raising a black child in the twenty-first century will be an uphill battle; however, the quality of sex education is the key to combating immature sexual behaviors.

Sex Education

Some of the most popular topics in sex education are abstinence and abortion. However, most African American parents skirt around real issues regarding sex. Their method of communication could be summed up in one word: "Don't." For example, they may say, "Don't believe everything you see on TV; don't come home pregnant; don't have sex without a condom; don't be like your mother or father who was a teen parent." Moreover, other black parents and immediate caregivers engage in sex education employing euphemisms. The psychology behind this approach is a desperate effort to lessen an overwhelming sense of anxiety. Parents tend to speak in code, such as substituting the words *sexual intercourse* with "it" or *penis* with "thing." Both parents and child typically feel awkward and embarrassed. This is particularly the situation with parents or immediate caregivers from the Depression era and baby boom generations.

As aforementioned, the best method to minimize anxiety is to begin informing the child about sex as early as possible, when he or she asks the first questions about babies or about sex organs. Since they don't require lengthy explanations, a simple matter-of-fact reply to a child's questions could be the beginning of a future healthy rapport.

There are parents, both married and single, who perform a miraculous job providing their children with effective sex information. The one common theme that these individuals possess is consistency. Also, they use various resources to expose their children to the consequences of early sex, honesty about sex early in development, and the benefits of waiting for sex regardless of peer pressure and media influence.

Equally important, African American children of single parents sometimes learn invaluable information in terms of sex education from their parents. They may grow up in a household where very little quality time is available, or they witness their parent working two or three jobs and decide that this isn't the life they desire to live. In many respects, children learn firsthand the challenges of providing for children, and they may come to realize that it's a situation that only mature adults can handle. It may influence them to delay sex until adulthood or marriage. Therefore in this instance, seeing could become believing.

Staying Two Steps Ahead of the Game

AFRICAN AMERICAN PARENTS MUST FIRST understand that sex education is an ongoing process that involves the whole family. Parents upholding traditional values of their generation can hinder effective sex education. The worst-case scenario—teen pregnancy—is a fear most parents harbor. Unplanned pregnancies are difficult realities in all African American communities: inner cities, suburbs, or rural sectors of the country. Many black females, who are often emotionally detached from either one or both biological parents, feel they must be validated by some boy desiring them or loving them. Thus they become fair game for any gamer. The young male will assess and perceive her as a "ho" or as "easy" or himself as being God's gift to her. Then he concludes that he must give her what she needs. This rationalizing triggers a series of events that can result in a form of sexual abuse.

Young females need to be made aware of the game of both younger and older males. In essence, there is a sexual crisis exploited by the media, propagated by fairy tales like *Cinderella*, and true-love publications where engaging in sex is confused with making love and being rescued by their knight. They rationalize the act with distortions of love viewed on television, one of the most powerful social influences, where the characters do not mention birth control, do not report inappropriate behavior, or consider consequences. The youth, being highly impressionable, essentially model perceived behaviors.

Young African American males don't normally suffer the romantic notions of their counterparts, but they need programming regarding games young females run on them: becoming pregnant to tie the baby's father to them with the ultimate goal of marriage, or aggressively pursuing a possible moneymaker and feigning career goals with the objective of seeking a young man to take care of them regardless of his moneymaking potential. Although the black female also desires sex, she often plays a more subtle role in pursuing it, allowing the male to believe he is the initiator—the aggressor.

What Lowers Risk of Teen Sex

THERE IS NO ONE-SIZE-FITS-ALL BLUEPRINT in the African American community geared for lowering risk factors to prevent teen sex. Parents and immediate caregivers historically have relied on methods of sex education passed down through their parents; some rely upon the school system; some conclude that their children will figure things out when they're mature enough. However, recent research suggests that African American parents who were successful at reducing preadolescent sex all had one thing in common—direction.

As simple as this concept is, too many African Americans don't consider it. Many factors play into this phenomenon; for instance, the age of the parents and socioeconomic status, to name two. According to Dr. Reisser (1993), several factors regarding direction contribute to delaying teen sex:

- Both parents in the home (particularly the biological father)
- Strong educational accomplishment/commitment to school
- Religious devotion
- A peer group that maintains strong advocacy of abstinence
- Community and parental values that support sex after marriage

- Host of goals and aspirations to become outstanding leaders of the future (opportunities for traveling, sports, academic honors, mentorships, apprenticeships, etc.)

Again, there is no panacea for encouraging African American youth to delay sex. An important element that's needed is close bonds between the youth and their parents. Also, parents must hold realistic expectations of them.

For parents and caregivers who aren't comfortable discussing sex, there's plenty of literature that can be secured from libraries, community centers, and schools. Black youth should also be schooled that unprotected sexual relationships or promiscuity can lead to communicable diseases and infections—another reason to delay sexual relationships.

Communicable Sexual Infections and Diseases

SEXUALLY TRANSMITTED DISEASES (STDs), ALSO known as sexually transmitted infections, are caused by organisms that can be transmitted from one person to another through sexual activity and intimate contact. According to the National Institute of Health there are more than 20 types of STDs. STDs can be categorized into two types—viral and bacterial. Viral STDs can only be treated not cured usually with anti-viral medication, freezing, burning or laser surgery. Conversely, bacterial STDs can be cured usually with an antibiotic. However, most STDs can be very dangerous to ones health primarily because some people show no signs or symptoms until weeks after sexual contact or intercourse.

Below are descriptions of several of the most common STDs.

Common Male Signs

Danger Signs

Discharge from penis, soreness inside penis, burning with urination, rectal irritation and pus, swelling or redness of throat, yellow discharge from penis

Could Be

Gonorrhea, NGU, other genital infections that also need medical attention

Complications

Untreated gonorrhea can cause sterility, arthritis, heart trouble, and blindness. Repeated infections can cause partial or complete blockage of the penis.

Common Female Signs

Danger Signs

Gray offensive vaginal discharge, thick and profuse vaginal discharge, intense itching, painful intercourse, thick cheesy discharge, rectal irritation and pus covering feces, swelling or redness of throat, out-of-cycle stomach cramps, unusual vaginal or cervical bleeding.

Could Be

Chlamydia, gonorrhea, nonspecific vaginitis, trichomoniasis, monilia (yeast), HPV (human papillomavirus, genital warts (a strain of HPV).

Complications

If untreated, gonorrhea can cause pelvic inflammatory disease, which resembles appendicitis. This causes severe pain, fever, sterility, arthritis, and heart trouble. If chlamydia is untreated, sterility may result. HPV may cause precancerous cells in the cervix.

Common Signs for Both Sexes

Danger Signs

Painful sore on penis or vagina, painful sore or blisters on or around genital area, rash on hands and feet or entire body, loss of hair, small cauliflower-pink growths on or around sex organs, intense itching, flu-like feeling.

Could Be

Syphilis, herpesvirus, hepatitis, scabies, crabs, genital warts (HPV)

Complications

Untreated syphilis can cause brain and other organ damage; also paralysis, heart disease, blindness, and death. The most severe complication of herpes genitalis is the infection of a newborn during birth, which can be fatal.

Courtesy of Florida State Department of Health and Rehabilitative Services.

Sexual Abuse

ALTHOUGH TEENAGE PREGNANCY IS NORMALLY undesired, there is some good news regarding it. According to CDC's National Center for Health Statistics (final data in 2002) "teen birth rate declined by 30 percent over the past decade to a historic low and that the rate for black teens was down by more than 40 percent." Although teen births are down in the African American community, a different type of sex is occurring at epidemic levels, which is seldom discussed—sexual abuse, of which the perpetrators are often people least expected.

Child sexual abuse can be best defined as any kind of sexual contact between an adult or older teen and a child. This behavior is used to gain power over the child and often involves a betrayal of the child's trust according to Licensed Marriage, Family Therapist Carol Boulware, Ph.D. (2006). She claims that sexual abuse ranges from body grabbing to touching sexual organs, masturbation, and making the child touch the adult sexually. Author Kathleen C. Faller (2003) defines sexual abuse as any act occurring between people who are at different developmental stages which is for the sexual gratification of the person at the more advanced developmental stage.

Specific Types of Sexual Abuse

1. Noncontact sexual abuse. This form of sexual abuse is made up of three types and involves no physical touching.

    A. A) Sexy talk. Here, sexual perpetrators make statements pertaining to the child's physical attributes. It is not unusual to hear the perpetrator confess to degrading sexual acts that he or she would like to engage in with the victim. Examples are as follows: "I want to fuck you," "I want you to suck my dick."

B. B) Exposure. This type of sexual abuse entails perpetrators exposing their naked bodies. They will often use their hands and make particular reference to their privates (i.e., breast, vagina, penis, or anus). Masturbation is also typical here.

C. C) Voyeurism. This behavior includes episodes of a perpetrator either covertly or overtly watching the victim while they are undressing, which provides the perpetrator with sexual gratification: watching a child take a bath, watching an infant's diaper change, or watching a child take a shower or even using the toilet.

2. Sexual contact. Involves any touching of the covered body parts: buttocks, anus, penis, vagina, breasts, and perinea vicinity. Perpetrators will frequently fondle their victims in a manner that manipulates the victims to reciprocate the behavior to the perpetrator. Fondling can occur on top or underneath the victim's clothes.

3. Oral genital sex. This behavior is characterized by any sexual activity involving the tongue, lips, or mouth to stimulate a person's erogenous zones and genitals by licking, sucking, biting, and/or kissing.

4. Interfemoral intercourse. This behavior is masturbation by moving the penis between the (lubricated) upper thighs of a child. This can be done in four different ways: (1) with a child standing or reclining, (2) with a child sitting on one's lap, (3) with a child lying on a bed or table with legs in the air, (4) by holding the child by the ankles in an upside down position.

5. Sexual penetration. Penetration involves acts of sodomy. It is an act, however slight, of sexual intercourse, cunnilingus, fellatio, anal intercourse, or any intrusion, however slight, of any part of the body or of any object into the genital or anal openings of another person's body.

6. Sexual exploitation (pimping or prostituting a child).

7. Sexual abuse in combination with other abuse.

Sexual abuse among African American children is huge, but it is difficult to find adequate statistics. Most of the research done on child sexual abuse does not include African Americans. However, clinical psychologists and professors at UCLA have proved the exceptions. Wyatt's research reflects variables such as race and culture in survivors' experiences. Wyatt states, "We're certainly not the only group that's silent regarding abuse. But we're the only group whose experience is compounded by our history of slavery and stereotypes about black sexuality, and that makes discussion more difficult" (Stone, 2004, p. 15). African American children who have been victimized or know someone who has been victimized should be taught to inform their parents or caregivers, and counseling should be sought. Equally important, parents and caretakers should take seriously allegations made by their children.

Sexual abuse is not confined to one socioeconomic group—it transcends all racial, gender, economic, and social boundaries. There is evidence that suggests that sexual abuse is more prevalent among children in lower-income families. This is partly true, because low-income families tend to have more contact with public agencies and authorities and may be observed more. Author Robin Stone (2004) suggests that public professionals such as teachers and doctors tend to be more vigilant of suspect abuse in economically challenged families. Nevertheless, affluent families who have less contact with social service agencies depend more on private family physicians. Oftentimes, when sexual abuse is detected in these situations, well-paid physicians may look the other way rather than acting upon their suspicions.

How Sexual Abuse Is Allowed to Exist in the Black Community

EXTENDED KINSHIPS HAVE ALWAYS PLAYED an important role in African American culture. This tradition has historically been an integral part of the children's socialization. The many extended kinships—aunts, cousins, uncles, and grandparents—are fundamental to African American children's development. This support system provides encouragement with the children's endeavors: basic education, school activities, sports activities, basic relationships, and orientation to sex. From this support system, young people learn what their immediate parents or caregivers aren't able to teach them, such as playing musical instruments, gardening, possibly skills involving relationships, or even endorsing high school and college aspirations. Above all, an understood code of trust is taken for granted amongst African American parents and caregivers. However, this trust is breached when a family member violates a child.

Some broken families that are already mired in common family problems, such as deficiency of funds and lack of employment or low-paying employment, may be less likely to investigate a suspicion or an allegation that their child has been molested. Regardless of economic status, some families will simply deny the possibility. To couple this with little to no communication in a family unit is a condition for sexual abuse to exist undetected under the radar. There is no single answer for this issue, but open and honest dialogue between parents and their children regarding appropriate or inappropriate behavior with others is pertinent.

Black children learn quickly that they are not always the center of attention in their immediate surroundings. They learn that in order to be heard, particularly after being subjected to sexual abuse, they must act out. Most sexually abused children will not disclose the known and trusted person that betrayed them. Shame and guilt and fear are the usual reasons given.

The children consumed with shame feel they did something wrong; the abuse was their fault. Likewise, it is not uncommon for parents or immediate caregivers to feel shame for denying accusations of sexual abuse perpetrated by someone they have grown to love and trust.

Fear can be as devastating as shame or guilt. Victims fear what abusers may do to them or a loved one. In fact, most sex abusers silence their victims by threatening them or family members with bodily harm. Victimized children are also reluctant to disclose the abuse due to their own nebulous thoughts—the mounting guilt regarding their role in the act or guilt related to possibly deriving pleasure.

Understanding Silence in the African American Community

THE IMPACT OF SLAVERY, AS well as the failure to learn from history, cannot be overlooked here. During the colonial period, black women were constantly raped by those in authority (masters) and at times were left by their mates to fend for themselves. Shouldering these burdens earned black women the title of noble victim. They mastered a coping silence in the wake of adversity that has been passed down through generations. According to psychologist Brenda Wade, "Our ancestors had to learn how to cope in order to survive the raw brutality and utter misery of slavery. Many of their coping strategies obviously served them well, because we're still here as a people; but in return, they paid an enormous psychological price, and today, we're still paying the interest. To survive, our ancestors learned to act complacent and submissive, in a sense putting on a mask to navigate through life. In fact, when defending or talking about sexual attacks by masters or other whites could lead to punishment such as lashing, being sold, or even death, the silence of black women became a sign of strength and determination not to allow such experiences to dominate the mind" (Stone, 2004, p. 27).

Today, employing this form of strength can lead to mental illness, a cycle of sexual abuse, and depression among African American children and youth. This same coping mechanism is noted in the book *Shifting: The Double Lives of African American Women*, mentioned earlier. African American children and youth in turn model their mothers' behavior and mimic this tactic. The youth and even adults silently enduring and suffering sexual abuse is a negative consequence; therefore, given the history of the survival tactics of African Americans, it is a painful truth that the same phenomenon that put them at ease around white folks is the same problem that positions them at risk for sexual abuse. Until the shifting concept is explained to our youth, especially girls—about how and when it's necessary—more of them will succumb to its ambiguous programming.

Messages such as, "Our bodies are not our own," teach African American youth to be submissive to all adults. Culturally-specific slogans such as, "I brought you into this world, and I can take you out," serve to reinforce submissive behavior toward adults, which includes sexual perpetrators. Often, parents instruct children to hug uncles, cousins, or brothers-in-law against their will. The underlying message to children is that they have no voice or say regarding their body; subsequently, their comfort and security must take a backseat to an adult's sexual gratification.

This self-defeating mode of thinking is changing; a few vanguard black parents are cognizant of the ramifications of insisting their children show affection against their will. Also, these parents are including a dialogue about what their children should do when touched inappropriately or propositioned. Some parents and immediate caregivers are allowing their children to be seen and heard, and are encouraging them to speak up to authority in appropriate situations.

Male Victims of Sexual Abuse

FAR TOO OFTEN WHEN WE think of child sexual abuse, females come to mind. There is seldom a dialogue on preteen and teen male victimization. As sensitive and complex as this topic is, factoring in the variable of culture adds to the complexity of the matter. In black culture, male sexual abuse is taboo because of deep-seated homophobia; consequently, males rarely receive adequate education in this regard, and more importantly, black males don't have safe places to resort to regarding their abuse. Also, African American males are conditioned to remain silent—it's the manly thing to do.

Be a Man

AMERICAN CULTURE PASSIONATELY TEACHES BOYS in general to maintain masculinity and suppress characteristics of femininity: sensitivity and creativity. This powerful message is reinforced in society and by mass media. Many African American parents and immediate caregivers also advocate it. For decades, American culture has subjected boys in general who displayed traits of nonmasculine behaviors to degrading labels, such as pussy, bitch, punk, faggot, wimp, and sissy. As a result, young black males are bombarded with these messages from infancy through adulthood. They, in turn, model other black youth and men. They learn to hide any feelings of vulnerability, thus stifling emotional growth, self-awareness, and willingness to disclose personal or intimate issues.

There's an unwritten code in the black community that says snitching is not cool. In fact, breaching this unwritten code is equated with treason in inner cities. Given this negative connotation, especially in inner cities, African American boys often feel uneasy about informing a parent or immediate caregiver of being sexually abused. Equally important, open dialogue about sexual abuse is difficult to anticipate for African American youth when their homes become an extension of what society maintains as standards of manhood. If the child's mother is the type that will call the son a punk or faggot for crying or seeking help with bullies, he most likely will learn to internalize and mask his problems. Michael Eric Dyson's essay "Behind the Mask" maintains that "many brothers have become so used to using masks to hide the injuries we've sustained doing battle with society that we lose our grip on who we really are" (Stone, 2004, p. 151). Dyson believes that in order for the home to be a safe haven, women will need to readjust their expectations: "Sisters, you often say you want a sensitive man, but when a brother shows his insecurities and fears, you worry that he's going to punk out" (Stone, 2004, p. 151).

Effects of Sexual Abuse

THE CONTRASTS OF THE EFFECTS between female and male abuse are largely influenced by society's expectations of manhood. Girls frequently experience guilt, powerlessness, sadness, hopelessness, isolation, denial, and self-destruction. Boys, on the other hand, coupled with what society tells them about being a man, grapple with these issues:

- Concerns about sexuality
- Concerns about masculinity
- Isolation
- Disclosing the abuse to others
- Feelings of inadequacy and vulnerability
- Recognizing abuse and its effects
- Finding resources and support

Sexually abused boys avoid reporting abuse for two primary reasons: being perceived as weak, and fear of being labeled homosexual. Moreover, therapists often cite, "Am I gay?" and "Will telling someone about it make everybody think that I'm gay?" as questions that most male survivors inquire about in therapy.

In many respects, African American parents and immediate caregivers have inadvertently conditioned their sons to be emotionally detached from their families and society. Many sexually abused young black males who have never received treatment will become abusers as adults. In fact, one study shows that 97 percent of offenders who committed violent crimes against children were male, and that violent child-victimizers were substantially more likely than adult-victimizers to have been physically or sexually abused as children. An analysis of studies found that abused males were more likely to sexually abuse others (Stone, 2004, p. 153). Again, this is partly the result of societal conditioning and messages—silence and virtually no safe haven to report sexual abuse without the fear of negative repercussions.

Another aspect of male abuse is that there appears to be a correlation between sexual abuse and domestic violence. Recent research suggests that males who physically abuse their wives have issues with their mothers. According to clinical psychologist Victoria J. Sloan, men "talk about their mothers who stayed with the man who brutally raped or abused them and sometimes even witnessed it, but didn't stop it. These men will have a lot of rage toward the women who didn't protect them" (Stone, 2004, p. 157).

The taboo topic of sexual abuse is suppressed in general because both parent and child are ill-equipped to deal with it. African Americans have been in denial regarding the occurrence of sexual abuse within the community far too long. The abuse of children and youth can no longer be rationalized as something that occurs just in the white community.

Old mores and taboos must be destroyed with aggressive programs to reeducate the youth and parents, and they must begin in the home.

CHAPTER 8

Money Philosophies

AFRICAN AMERICAN MONEY MANAGEMENT HABITS and the effects they have on their offspring is an intriguing topic, and there is very little material published on the matter. Far too many children are exposed to inadequate, inappropriate, and irresponsible money management. Most African Americans would agree that economic mobility is indeed feasible, but too few actually possess blueprints to achieve this goal. "Today's native born African Americans once descended from people who, as slaves, were deracinated from their native cultures. This de-culturation has been one of the key factors impeding the economic advancement of the African American community in the United States" (Fukuyama, 1996, p. 296). Indeed, the impact of slavery and its acute repercussions has had an influence on African American families and their children. However, their self-defeating money practices, particularly by those who have not been exposed to money management education, serve as an affirmation that they are not failures, but students who are still learning. Throughout this chapter, financial management, financial literacy, and money management will be discussed interchangeably as they relate to the socialization of the African American child.

According to the Black Diaspora Magazine (2001), African Americans spend more than 400 billion dollars annually. This money is allotted to food, credit cards, insurance, gifts, clothing, utilities, car payments, mortgages, and entertainment. First, one must begin with the more salient irresponsible money spending habit—excessive credit card usage.

Ideally, credit card spending should be utilized primarily for emergency situations; however, they're also used to purchase clothes, jewelry, computers, groceries, dining, and entertainment, often on a daily basis. Credit card holders receive programming via television and other media to spend as much as desired and pay later. The credit card industry thrives on consumers spending *by any means necessary*, while attaching skyrocketing interest rates and finance charges to their accounts.

Warning signs of irresponsible spending are always there, but are often ignored: notices of maximized credit limits, receiving late-payment notices or phone calls from creditors and juggling payments—that is, using one card to make payment on another. As adults lead this credit card fiasco, their children are learning from their example.

In Kevin Boston's book *Smart Money Moves for African Americans,* (1997) he advocates the concept of African Americans building their net worth. Boston defines net worth as the remainder after all liabilities are subtracted from all assets. Ironically, one strategy of building net worth is with credit cards. Available credit should be used to purchase an education, antiques, works of art, homes, rental property, securities, and businesses. Boston recommends these acquisitions because they are appreciating assets and will increase one's net worth. Moreover, Boston suggests additional wealth-building strategies, such as securing term/disability insurance plans, entrepreneurship, home ownership, and investing in the stock market. Children can be encouraged to begin by opening a savings account.

Early Interventions for Youth When Moving Out of the House

ONE OF MANY CONSPICUOUS CRISES in the African American community is the lack of early adulthood preparation for managing an apartment or a house. Many children—namely, those in early adulthood—experience firsthand that running a household is similar to operating a business.

Paying utilities, buying food, purchasing miscellaneous products, allotting funding for home maintenance, making car payments, and setting aside money for insurance, rent, or a mortgage are essential tasks. Parents and caregivers alike often believe that rearing a child toward independence is assisting them with a college or vocational/technical school but leaving money management to chance. As a result, African American children, along with many other children in America, upon reaching adulthood tend to fail horribly at maintaining households and other adult responsibilities. It is important to note that there are a few exceptions to the norm; there are young people who successfully manage their finances and lives.

The amounts of income that single parents or two-parent families earn will ultimately dictate how much funding will be disbursed on bills. When it is time to pay utilities, the child or children should be brought to the table and the bill-paying process should be explained. Of course, a few young people who are forced to pull their weight with jobs gain firsthand knowledge of income and expense management.

Most American households share a notion that when a youth turns eighteen, he or she is grown and should be ready for adult responsibilities— securing and maintaining a job or an education, and possibly an apartment. Although many aren't able to, some that are successfully living independently of their parents or financial sponsors realize that it takes discipline, skill, and savvy.

Indeed, being oblivious to money management gives rise to an economic vacuum, which is filled by those who possess a higher money management IQ. Living in a predatory society automatically sets up poor money managers for failure—to be exploited. In short, someone else is going to dictate his or her financial future.

Most households have someone designated to pay bills and to purchase food and dry goods. Similarly, there should be a strategy for developing a child's financial IQ—someone planning and budgeting alongside the child until the procedure is learned. Parents who have to juggle monthly bills should explain to their children the circumstances for this issue. Indeed, children can learn two lessons from this practice—spend less or earn more.

A proactive approach is to encourage children to provide an income from enterprises such as yard services or recycling aluminum cans in their community or babysitting or dog walking. The goal would be to broaden children's vision of entrepreneurial possibilities, which would also provide them with money management experiences. By the same token, creating a small business at an early age will teach basic skills in pricing, accounting, communication, customer satisfaction, and marketing. Later, these skills could be extended into a viable enterprise.

Children who are provided allowances should be held accountable for their expenditures. All young people should be encouraged to save.

According to the Jump Start Coalition for Personal Financial Literacy (JCPFL; 2008), a group founded in 1997 to promote personal finance education, high school students' money management IQ has declined in recent years. The debt accumulation of many young folks is indicative of this fact. Experts explain that money management habits solidify by middle school to high school for all children. Although the JCPFL study was not relegated to a particular race, it demonstrates the importance of implementing a systematic money management regime with children when they're young. Most African American households are financially illiterate—systematically yielding to a pattern of perpetual debt. Therefore, parents and immediate caregivers must instill new vantage points and possibilities in their children's psyches.

Mothers, after hearing about the JCPFL program, frequently inquire if their children have the tools necessary to comprehend the concept of money management. According to Jean Piaget (1991), a pioneer in children's cognitive development, children, ages two to six, develop the attainment of conservation of numbers and intuitive problem solving. If Piaget theory is valid, then a child-friendly model for investing is in order. Susan Beacham, ex-banker and mother of two, created the Money Savvy Pig, a see-through bank with slots for saving, spending, investing, and donating. This model should be introduced throughout the black community as an alternative. The hope is to begin their financial literacy training early enough so that good money management becomes a habit.

Additional money management efforts that show promise are emerging in the black church. As grim as this epidemic may appear, divinely inspired efforts are being made to counter this setback. A movement that has its roots in the religious community has accepted the challenge of teaching financial literacy with an objective of producing a smarter, competent, well-prepared, financially literate African American child. This is an ingenious strategy of members of the African American community pooling their resources and doing for themselves. This example demonstrates measures needed to revolutionize African American culture in order to determine the destiny of their youth's economic development.

Author Amy Marcus reports, "During the past decade, African Americans did not invest in stocks at anything near the rates that whites did (64 percent vs. 82 percent, according to a study by Ariel Mutual Funds and Charles Schwab)" (*Money*, August 2001, p. 99). Consequently, pastors are working with the advocacy organization Rainbow PUSH Coalition (see *The Gospel of Money* article). Investment clubs are becoming en vogue across both denominational and racial lines. More specifically, the yearning for financial literacy appears to be deeper than a cultural issue; instead, recent evidence suggests that it's a human issue.

Ministers invited by Rainbow PUSH attended a three-day investing seminar hosted by the New York Stock Exchange. The invaluable information attained was then channeled to congregational members, where it really counted. Other churches have often invited consultants to speak directly to their congregations. Both tactics share a common goal of teaching financial literacy. However, smaller congregations have not yet embraced this practice.

Far too many black families are sentencing their children to perpetual debt, courtesy of a day-to-day mentality. The survival instinct is no less important than it was during slavery, but today there is more access to free education. Like all other privileges and freedoms, responsibility comes with it, and African Americans who buy into the system will most likely assume the responsibility of sound money management policies.

College and Money

PARENTS WHO CHOOSE TO REAR their children for college are no doubt aware of the cost. College tuition is expected to increase by an average of 4.5 to 6.5 percent a year depending on the institution according to The Chronicle of Higher Education 2009. Teaching a black youth to understand the link between preparation and soaring college tuition is necessary at an early age. For starters, allowances, gifts, and money set aside by parents are excellent resources for beginning a college fund. Assets become more valuable over periods of time. Ariel Mutual Funds has a slogan, "Slow and Steady Weathers the Storm," which is particularly important for paying for college or vocational school, if the parent begins the fund early enough. If not, the youth must depend upon grants and loans supplemented by part-time employment.

Spirituality and Money

IN THE BIBLE, MATTHEW 19:24 reads, "It is easier for a camel to go through the eye of a needle, than for a rich man to enter into the kingdom of God." This ancient proverb is interpreted in a myriad of ways by what is known as hermeneutics—the science and methodology of interpretation, especially of the Bible.

The goal of this chapter is to encourage the creation of appropriate tools to assist black children to become skilled financial planners for their future. It is equally important to analyze the black community engaging in distortions and misinterpretations of biblically inspired concepts or scriptures that justify wealth restriction. These learned concepts too often sentence the youth to a permanent state of poverty. The following are a few poverty-promoting beliefs:

1. "Money is the root of all evil."

This biblical concept has and is undermining financial literacy in the African American community. The actual meaning of this erroneous slogan can be found in the book of Timothy as follows: "For the love of money is the root of all evil." In this case, the child may still erroneously conclude that striving for money is evil.

2. "I'll get my reward in heaven."

Ideally, black folks must look beyond the unknown, in terms of the biblical heaven, and deal with this heaven and hell on planet earth. Before parents and caregivers express their stance on money management, they should remember that they have an option of creating wealth for their children, which will make life as they know it heavenly, or they could continue to teach their children wishful thinking and poor money habits that will ultimately place them in hell on earth.

3. "My Social Security will take care of me."

This is a stage in which an individual is waiting to be saved. They are displacing personal responsibility onto someone or something else. Relying on financial institutions to help solve their financial problems is another way of saying, "I would appreciate it if someone else takes charge of my financial future." More importantly, this attitude is passed down to African American children, thereby perpetuating the cycle of social assistance dependency.

4. "You can't take it with you."

This sentiment is nothing short of another excuse to evade wealth building. Although it may have some validity because those who we leave behind—namely, the family—must continue to maintain the household, pay bills, and maintain a desired lifestyle; therefore, savings, trust funds, and life insurance are in order.

5. "My God will take care of me."

The proverb "God helps those who helps themselves" is thrown out the window. With the prior phrase, many African Americans believe that God will mysteriously rescue them from their financial woes. They sincerely believe that all they have to do is sit and wait and believe—have faith. They fail to take responsibility for themselves; they fail to manage their money, but often run to others for financial assistance and then sit back, proclaiming that "God took care of me."

Parents must equally understand that misinterpreting scriptures and justifying legacies of financial illiteracy will ultimately contribute to perpetuating a systematic underclass. Culturally speaking, spiritual capital is like outer space, in terms of its infinite potential. Until the African American community understands that money is an indispensable tool needed more in this life than in the afterlife, discussion in regard to spiritual capital will continue to emphasize the need for money in this life, as we know it.

Parents should solicit money management assistance from community centers, community colleges, libraries, or the Internet. The challenge is to persuade these parents and caregivers to change their attitudes and to embrace the opportunities money has allowed them and their offspring to enjoy and to begin wealth-building practices that will maintain or afford them a comfortable lifestyle.

The Balance of Needs and Wants

As DIFFICULT AS IT IS raising black children in a society that is obsessed with materialism, it is more difficult for the child if the parents are affected as well. A single parent who has very little family or extended family support may not have the energy to devote to teaching children money management; however, with effort she or he could become a model of prudent financial decisions.

One of the most common financial pitfalls is the inability to separate needs from wants. Human beings primarily need food, water, and shelter, and then love and affection. This can be further explored in Abraham Maslow's *Hierarchy of Needs* (Lundin, 1991). On the other hand, too many people who are materialistic have a tendency to run rampant with wants. In the African American child's mind, a want could be anything from a pair of Air Jordan shoes to a three-hundred-dollar bicycle. More often than not, the line between needs and wants becomes blurred when no sound example is made available for the youth to mimic. It is imperative that African American youth are made aware of the want/need phenomenon. Author Fran Harris (1998) suggests teaching black youth about needs and wants with the following exercise: First, take out a blank sheet of paper. Next, draw two columns, one for the child's needs, and the second column for the child's wants. This exercise should look similar to the following columns noted below:

Needs   **Wants**

_____   _____

_____   _____

_____   _____

After the child notes his or her answers, open the floor for questions and answers. Parents should not be quick to judge the child's choices. Oftentimes what may appear absurd to an adult is logical to the child. If a child includes a new car in his needs column, he may have wanted it for his mother, so that she doesn't have to struggle as much, possibly with bus schedules or taxi fares. This exercise is one of many for laying a foundation for children to become financially literate.

The Greatest Money Management Mistakes Black Parents Make with Their Children

Showering Children with Gifts

African American children, five to six years of age, have no real need for more than two gifts for their birthday. The message and expectation the parents are sending when they exceed this number of gifts is that the following years, the number will grow. Receiving multiple gifts can be overwhelming, especially if it's more than the child requested. The parents will set themselves up for failure; not only will the child want more with each ensuing birthday, they will be less likely to appreciate the abundance.

Giving Money to Children without Requiring Them to Earn It

No amount of money should be allotted to a child if he or she does not assume a degree of responsibility. If they are not taking out the trash or cleaning their room, or participating in other household chores, then rewarding them with an allowance may not be best. Ideally, a degree of responsibility and accountability should be established before disbursing money.

Teaching Children that Money Equals Success

This statement refers to parents or immediate caregivers boasting about someone's lofty salary. "Dr. Jones is all right. He makes two hundred thousand dollars a year." A better message to instill in the youth is that sound money management affords success.

Giving Kids the Impression that Money Is the Ultimate Goal

Statements such as, "If only I was making seventy-five thousand dollars, I'd be all right," or "If only I made more money, I wouldn't have these problems," send the wrong message. Young people should be taught that the ultimate goal should be to provide oneself with a productive and comfortable living by sound money management.

Saying "Do As I Say"

Like all children, African American children model behavior. There is a saying that suggests people should practice what they preach to the best of their ability. Parents who fail to conduct themselves in the manner they demand of their children send mixed messages. It will confuse the children, and as they grow older they may confront their parents' hypocrisy. If the parents or caregivers are choking with credit card debt, they can adopt the best debt-busting technique and apply it to their situation and hope that their children learn from their example.

Giving the Impression that Stuff Equals Love

Parents who substitute gifts for love should be cautioned. The elation that children experience is temporary. Once they come down off their high, they are left with a huge void. African American children need the physical presence of a parent or immediate caregiver to provide love and attention rather than stuff.

Failing to Use Every Opportunity to Teach Children Money Management

Parents or caregivers need to teach their offspring budgeting and saving habits, providing that they themselves possess them. When the youth splurges or makes unwise purchases, instead of verbally reprimanding him or her, a money management lesson should be presented.

Conducting One-Sided Financial Discussions

Households in which discussions of money are one-sided set the stage for poor money management. If a child asks for money, she is usually given a yes or a no reply. Parents or caregivers who respond in this manner leave no room for explanations why they were awarded or denied money.

Avoidance of the state of the finances when the child is requesting money could be crippling.

Not Allowing Children to Experience Money

Equally important, African American youth need to put their newly learned theories to practice. Parents who give allowances or use alternative methods of allotting money to their children need to allow them the freedom to apply their management skills and to encourage them to try again if they fail.

Assuming They Understand How Money Works

Parents and caregivers should not allow their children to believe that money is only needed for purchasing material items; it should be explained that it is also needed for funding public programs and institutional services such as the YMCA, Goodwill Industries, community-based breakfasts and lunch programs, and government agencies as well.

Fighting about Money in the Presence of Children without Any Explanation

Many parents and caregivers lack the understanding of how profoundly a heated argument about money can affect children's attitudes regarding money management habits; it may confuse them. Parents should either provide some explanations or argue it out behind closed doors.

The Biggest Mistakes Kids Make with Money

Overextending themselves

Borrowing from friends

Not being satisfied with what they have

Lending money

Not understanding the perceived power of money in the black community

Stashing all their money

Acquiring a Job

INDEPENDENCE IS A WORD THAT most African American youth can relate to, particularly when they reach the adolescent stage in their cognitive development. Acquiring their first taxable job, along with budgeting their pay, requires discipline and money management knowledge.

When a child chooses to work, one of the first questions or concerns a parent or immediate caregiver should have is the effect a job will have on their education. Parents should require verbal or written proposals explaining work hours and study hours. Plus the potential employee should be encouraged to save a percentage of the income.

In addition, African American youth should be made aware of the ugly side of the workforce: sexism, sexual harassment, racism, classism, bigotry, consequences of breaking the law, driving while black, respect for authority, professionalism, and double standards on all levels.

Internet Usage

NO OTHER INSTRUMENT IN HUMAN history has allowed people to communicate as efficiently as the Internet. Today, many people and organizations depend on its convenience, efficiency, and entertainment. With just a few taps of a button, one can communicate with anyone in the world. The Internet in the twenty-first century has become essential to everyday life itself.

However, there is currently a computer literacy gap in the African American community. Far too many African Americans would eagerly choose a luxury item in lieu of a computer. They particularly fail to understand its significance, especially for their children. For parents and caregivers who own a computer, exposing African American children to its possibilities will benefit them for life. Thanks to the Internet, personal finance has been revolutionized. In their book *It's About the Money*, Rev. Jesse L. Jackson, Sr., and Jesse L. Jackson, Jr., discuss the many ways the Internet contributes to the black people's financial literacy—the adults as well as the youth:

1. Create a budget and manage household finances.
2. Pay bills and do banking.

3. Do taxes.

4. Buy and sell stocks, bonds, and mutual funds very inexpensively.

5. Get reams of valuable investment advice.

6. Review the balance in retirement accounts such as a company's 401(k).

7. Find the best-priced mortgage lender and interest rates for a home loan.

8. Compare the performance of different mutual funds.

9. Purchase insurance.

10. Find a job.

11. Go shopping.

12. Get an accredited university or graduate degree, such as an MBA or degree in computer science, online via virtual instruction.

Credit Report

CHILDREN'S SCHOOL PERFORMANCE IS ASSESSED via a report card, usually consisting of five letter grades (A–F). Just as good grades and high marks are noted on the report card, children should be taught the same action is so with a credit report, a document that illustrates one's personal history of paying bills and how one manages their bill-paying history. Adolescent age would be the best time to begin this dialogue.

Parents should emphasize the necessity of paying bills by the due date with consistency if they want a good report. The youth need to understand how good grades on the credit report help to secure car loans, house loans, and even cell phones. It needs to be emphasized that without good credit, one may experience difficulty achieving the following:

- Being hired for a job

- Qualifying for a mortgage loan on a house

- Becoming eligible for a bank loan to start a new business

- Qualifying for a student loan to finance an education

- Buying a car

- Renting an apartment

- Obtaining a credit card

- Obtaining auto insurance or life insurance

- Arranging for gas or electric utility services in a home or an apartment

African American parents and caregivers must consistently stress to their children that a creditor can and will pull from one of three credit reporting agencies (Equifax, Trans Union, Experian) mentioned below to probe an individual's creditworthiness. This history will also determine what type of action the lender will pursue.

Penalties that individuals face with bad credit are higher interest rates on loans, and creditors will begin tracking a youth's payment history at age eighteen. With a fundamental understanding in financial literacy, they can avoid bad credit ratings and high interest rates and other pitfalls. Again, young people need to understand that good credit is essential for becoming independent and productive citizens. Good credit is necessary for black people to combat discrimination, although it may not eliminate it.

Credit scoring basically matches points to characteristics listed in an employment application. A credit reviewer makes a supposedly objective decision by way of the number of points an applicant scores. Moreover, credit scoring systems may also be programmed for computer analysis. An illustration of a simple credit scoring card is cited below.

Characteristic Point Value

Length of time at address
Less than two years 0
Two to five years 2
More than five years 3
Length of time on job
Less than two years on job/in field 0
Two to five years on job 1
Less than five years on job, two to five years in field 2
Five years or more on job/in field 4

Type of credit references
Finance company reference –1
No credit history 0
Retail card only 2
Bank card only 4
Bank card and retail card 5
Payment history
Collection, judgment, or suit –5
Late 30–120 days –2
Late 0–30 days 1
No late trades 5
13–17 points - Accept application, offer loan.
8–12 points - Obtain additional references before making decision.
7 or fewer points - Reject application.

Accessing a credit report can be done by either calling or writing one of three of the largest credit reporting agencies in the United States. Their contact information is listed as follows:

Equifax Information Service Center
Attention: Consumers Dept.
P.O. Box 105873
Atlanta, Georgia 30348
Phone: 1-800-658-1111

Trans Union Corporation
National Consumer Disclosure Center
P.O. Box 390
Springfield, Pennsylvania 19064-0390
Phone: 1-800-916-8800

Experian (formerly TRW)
P.O. Box 2104
Allen, Texas 75013-2104
Phone: 1-888-397-3742

Note: Obtaining a credit report can be free of charge or may cost up to eight dollars for a copy.

The importance of financial literacy and money management cannot be overstated. A parent can't begin too early to teach a child to save and plan their expenditures with the hope it becomes a life-long habit. It also must be instilled that it's not as important how much money they're able to generate as it is how well they manage it. The youth must realize that one day they'll want to purchase a house or apply for an apartment or purchase a car or apply for credit cards, all of which require good financial standing and money management skills. Establishing a strong financial foundation in African American children will greatly enhance their quality of life and ability to remain debt free.

CHAPTER 9

—▶ ◀—

Ebonics

EBONICS IS A LANGUAGE FORM, employing similar word and sound usage as the Negro dialect documented in poetry published by poets/authors James Edwin Campbell and Paul Lawrence Dunbar (1992) at the end of the eighteenth century and at the beginning of the nineteenth century.

The word *Ebonics* stems from two primary roots: Ebo, which comes from the term ebony, referring to dark or black; and phonics, a word referring to phonetics, the branch of language study dealing with sounds and symbols. Culturally speaking, Ebonics has its grammatical and structural roots in West African language systems, although some experts are in agreement that many white conservatives reduce Ebonics to a pseudo- and gutter language.

The most controversial Ebonics issue occurred in the Oakland, California, school district. The school board announced that its goal was to educate teachers in the district to speak Ebonics so that they could more effectively teach their students Standard English. Recent criticism provoked the Oakland School Board to reword the verbiage of the original Ebonics initiative. Especially puzzling was their original resolution's assertion that "African Language Systems are genetically based and not a dialect of English. Although the board issued a clarification that the word "genetically" was meant to indicate "origins," (as derived from the word "genesis") most have understandably interpreted it in biological terms (Hall, 1997). As innovative as this may appear, some educators, parents, and caregivers took issue with this strategy. In spite of their objections, the art of speaking Ebonics, or Black English, has always and will continue to be at the forefront of educating the African American child.

African American parents teach Ebonics to their children. This is not to suggest that all black parents speak this language form. Social status plays a critical part. However, unless black parents are well versed in Standard English, they may not be able to teach it.

Most behavioral theorists will agree that children master language by modeling adults. When a culture is intermingled with English grammar, a myriad of interpretations are certain to follow. For instance, some children may express being cold as "I be cold." The standard English version is "I am cold" or "I am really cold." The verb *be* is often substituted for the verbs *am* and *is*. In most cases, auxiliary verbs are dropped entirely, such as in the phrase, "He my daddy." Another example of this language form is "Don't fool wid me" or "Don't mess wid me," meaning "Don't bother me." The language is different to a degree in the description of the activity, but the communication is the same, which ultimately is the purpose of language.

Ebonics is spoken spontaneously where adults gather routinely to play cards, dominoes, or sports, or to watch games on TV, and children are afforded an indirect learning experience. The youth hear this cultural interpretation of English and consider it the standard. As a rule of thumb, the first of any orientation, especially language introduced to a child, is usually accepted as the norm.

In addition to African American children learning Ebonics from their parents, mass media promote it as well. Pop culture, particularly hip-hop (which is the most powerful/influential music today) and movies, promote Ebonics' themes. Hip-Hop artists Ice Cube, 50 Cent, Jay-Z. Das Efx, Nas, and Snoop Dogg draw upon Ebonics quite frequently in their music. It is a reflection of the hip-hop artists' heritage. To embrace Ebonics as an artist is usually an affirmation of their culture—of their socialization. African American youth who embrace Ebonics are also embracing their heritage. Parents, educators, and caregivers should not discourage it, no matter how uncomfortable they are with Ebonics. African American children possess more than enough genius to master it and Standard English, as well as several other languages.

Most individuals who are fluent in Ebonics will note that it is incomplete without the appropriate pronunciation and syntax. Author Edward T. Hall noted a similar idea in the following: "There is a sound system for any language and ... the speakers are bound by the system of their own language. This is why the first language one learns exerts an influence over all subsequent ones and gives them an accent" (Hall, 1973, p. 114).

As mentioned previously, there tends to be a link between Ebonics and social class. Those of lower socioeconomic rank equate Black English as an authentic barometer of what is known as being real. It has always been a part of the human experience for people to find safety in numbers. The purpose of Ebonics was and is for effective communication within African American culture. It is no different than Native Americans speaking their native tongue among themselves.

One of the misconceptions in people who know little about black culture is that they think all people who look physically black speak Ebonics, which is far from the truth. Most African American children know that Ebonics is not accepted in American society. Black youth learn as soon as they enter public and private schools that Ebonics is a devalued speech pattern.

How Parents Can Assist Teachers

THE RESPECT FOR AND UNDERSTANDING of a first language form cannot be solely the responsibility of the classroom teacher. Teacher aides and parents can support the instructional process and assist black children's language development in general by the following:

- Encouraging children to speak in a variety of situations and before many audiences
- Establishing talking as a frequent, enjoyable, and secure activity
- Modeling and expanding students' speech into language appropriate for the topic, situation, and audience
- Pointing out what language and communicative behaviors are appropriate as situations occur
- Discouraging teasing about speech

- Not overcorrecting students' speech

- Linking corrections of speech to the situation

- Providing the school and teacher with examples of speech used in the home and community to incorporate in instruction, assessment, and teacher training

- Reinforcing writing or reading with activities that include talking

- Providing an abundance of verbal stimuli for students irrespective of language or communication competencies

- Encouraging students to engage in conversations with a variety of people and on a variety of subjects

- Encouraging students to recount their experiences in narrative form as often as possible and before a variety of audiences

Walking Dictionaries

THE POSSIBILITY OF A FORMAL Ebonics dictionary is a looming debate. Two authoritative guides were discovered: Clarence Major's 548-page *Jaba to Jive: A Dictionary of African American Slang* (1994; a revised, expanded version of his 1970 *Dictionary of Afro-American Slang*), and Geneva Smitherman's 243-page *Black Talk: Words and Phrases from the Hood to the Amen Corner* (a revised and expanded edition was issued in 2000). In addition, there have been many scholarly articles or lengthy studies published regarding Ebonics dictionaries.

In recent times, however, African American youth, primarily in urban and rural areas, created a vast list of terms associated with Ebonics. Regardless of formal documentation in a book, these youngsters produce terms that can be translated and articulated in Standard English. For instance, the term *playa hatta* means to tarnish one's reputation in African American culture. Conversely, in Standard English, the translation of playa hatta means denigration: to damage the character or reputation of someone. This term, like so many other Ebonics terms, changes rapidly. Others like "I be cold" will remain. Each generation will coin a set of words with some meaning unique to their experience.

The Alienated African American Child

AFRICAN AMERICAN CHILDREN WHO ARE raised in predominately white neighborhoods and schools often view themselves as outsiders when in the company of Ebonics-speaking children. These difficult and painful experiences often leave the non-Ebonics-speaking children feeling alienated or feeling that something is wrong with them. When both black and nonblack children are totally oblivious to African American history, it makes it difficult to psychologically reference a living or historic African American figure who spoke Standard English. Youth who are exposed early will most likely make the connection needed to embrace Standard English. Contemporary cinema and pop media have placed prominent African American figures aforementioned as role models. However, their productions in which Black English is used are only welcomed if they're entertaining. These figures can be seen on popular sitcoms shows such as the *Dave Chappelle Show* or *In Living Color*. Regardless of the limiting manner in which the dominant culture accepts Black English, African American youth who only speak it must eventually master Standard English in order to succeed in the 21st Century.

When Teachers Devalue Ebonics

AFRICAN AMERICAN CHILDREN WHO ATTEND public schools with little mastery of Standard English are involved with a host of problems that impede age-appropriate learning. Teachers who lack the cultural sensitivity—namely, understanding and accepting Ebonics—meet these students with stoic denial of the validity of their culture. At the earliest stages, their first language is considered bad. As a result, African American children experience a psychological wedge between themselves and the teachers. In author Gail Thompson's book *Through Ebony Eyes: What Teachers Need to Know But Are Afraid to Ask About African American Students*, she cited a quote by Delpit: "To speak out against the language that children bring to school means that we are speaking out against their mothers, that their mothers are not good enough to be a part of the school world" (Thompson, 2004, p. 142).

Public school teachers who overcorrect Ebonics-speaking black youth risk alienating already troubled students, for sure. They're usually the last to ask questions and participate in class discussions.

Many teachers associate Ebonics with ignorance, inferiority, foolishness, and lower socioeconomic status rather than respecting it as a critical tie that links speakers of this dialect to their communities. Nonetheless, two things must take place before an effective change can occur: the public school system will have to be reformed and parents will have to make an effort to retrain themselves and their children to include learning Standard English. Their language of birth is not enough to fully function in this society. Ideally, the classroom milieu should be conducive to embracing Ebonics-speaking African American children. This would certainly help minimize the number of children who are slipping through the cracks; however, the Ebonics debate is only a minute portion of the larger issue—the denial of a segment of African American culture.

CHAPTER 10

——➤ ◀——

Divorce

IN RECENT YEARS, THE BREAKDOWN of family that has permeated America—number one in the world for divorce—is largely due to all the negative aspects of the information age. The reality of divorce is that it has a devastating effect upon adults as well as their children. Oftentimes, adults would like to think that divorce will have a minor impact upon a child's life, but current research suggests otherwise. The degree of emotional damage sustained largely depends on their age and stage of cognitive development.

According to Kay M. Porterfield, author of *Straight Talk About Divorce*, since 1960, America's divorce rate has tripled: "In 1995 alone, nearly 62 million couples in the United States ended their marriages." Given past and current statistics on divorce, one should ponder possible reasons so many couples choose to divorce.

During the past forty-five years, external forces have been systematically working to undermine family values in America. To an extent, the same forces affecting Hispanic and white families are impacting African American families. According to Besharov and West, elements that seem to work against the black family are, "the devastating effects of slavery and Jim Crow laws on black marriage; endemic poverty, which puts added stress on already weak families; even fewer gains from marriage, especially for women; too early sex that puts young girls at greater risk of unwanted pregnancy; and racial concentration that magnifies the impact of these conditions" (Besharov and West, 2000, p. 108). Moreover, shattered

African American families are forced to raise children in a rapidly changing world characterized by the technological revolution, premarital sex, more women gaining economic independence from men, and consumer-driven self-centered and materialistic values.

There is also less value placed on the environment, collective activity, and social responsibility. African American families who are currently grappling with these elements know from firsthand experience of the harsh realities that African American children face as a result of a broken family unit. Unlike any other period in U.S. history, more African American youth are on probation, on parole, incarcerated, shot and killed, or contacting HIV.

Since 1960, a disintegration of norms and values appears to be the underlying factor contributing to family breakdown. This factor is not only commonplace in the African American community; it apparently affects all families in American society.

Age-Specific Reactions to Divorce

THE SCOPE OF AGE-SPECIFIC REACTIONS to divorce is as follows: infancy and the toddler stage, grade school and early childhood, adolescence, and post-adolescence.

Infants, toddlers, and preschoolers are the most dependent of these groups. They are totally dependent on their parents and caregivers for food, shelter, love, and affection. Therefore, experiencing their parents divorcing catapults their once secure environment into chaos. Infants and toddlers tend to feel abandoned and to have their security threatened by the separation of their parents. They typically react in the following manner: they cry more frequently; they experience difficulty sleeping at night; they become more irritable; and they act out aggressively. Researchers have concluded that most of their reactions are rooted in the fear that if one parent leaves, the other will also.

The responses to divorce from children five to eight years old are mostly intuitive and quizzical. Their thought processes are developed enough to understand cause and effect; consequently, many African American children and other children in general feel extremely rejected and guilty as a result of perceiving themselves as the cause of the divorce. Children at this stage also frequently fantasize about their family reconciling their differences someday.

The impact of divorce at the adolescent stage promotes confrontational behaviors. Many parents recognize this behavior as acting out. Anger is there and can be manifested in a host of ways. One distinct pattern of blatant anger is directed at the parent whom the child perceives is at fault for the divorce. Therefore, if one parent is considered a villain, the other parent is considered worthy of loyalty, and children will choose the side of the non-villain or the person they perceive as faultless or the victim.

In addition, children ages nine and ten sometimes spy on the parent perceived as the villain out of rage and hurt. Long-lasting resentment develops when the unfavored parent enters into a new relationship; any hopes of reuniting the biological family are shattered.

Adolescents who were once burden free are sometimes thrust into adult roles when separation and divorce occur. The responsibility of caring for their siblings is often forced upon them, which could include preparing meals and attending to their siblings' personal hygiene.

Both parents and caregivers agree that adolescence is the most difficult stage of the African American child's development—regardless of divorce. Many changes occur in adolescents, such as an influx of hormones, identity searching, and growth spurts. This is also the period of transition from childhood to adulthood, at least physically. In addition, adolescents are in a state of self-doubt, questioning themselves as well as their immediate surroundings. Unlike the infants and toddlers, young children and grade school children, adolescents are searching for identity, which can manifest itself in succumbing to peer pressure, exploring sexuality, having run-ins with the law, and experimenting with drugs. In addition to all of these overwhelming pressures, there is a prevailing divorce with which they must contend. Parents or caregivers are normally the only constant the youth rely on during difficult times; however, during a divorce, that luxury is diminished or shattered.

It is suggested that divorced parents set and enforce strong values during this period. Adolescents are most likely to undergo a seesaw existence with guidelines and rules set by authority figures—biological parents and new spouses. If in the beginning they become rebellious, during the latter stages they eventually adopt the value system set by their parents.

Conversely, some adolescents after divorce manifest their rebelliousness in different manners or disengage from normal behavior altogether. Some of this depends upon the type of relationship the child has with his newly single separated parents.

Causal Factors of Divorce: The Word

THE WORD REFERS TO PASSAGES from the Bible and the relationship black people have with the church that affords them peace. Although black men and women are involved with the church, black women are the majority. In the book *Shifting: The Double Lives of Black Women in America*, authors Gooden and Jones maintain, "Based on a review of five national studies, Robert Joseph Taylor of the University of Michigan and his colleagues concluded that black people have stronger religious feelings than whites, and black women are more religious than black men" (Gooden and Jones, 2003, p. 260). Furthermore, per The Pew Forum on Religion & Public Life more than "eight-in-ten black women (84%) say religion is very important to them, and roughly six-in-ten (59%) say they attend religious services at least once a week." Most black women view the church as a sanctuary away from the "bitter hell" they face at home and in society.

Although not all black women act accordingly, some are so immersed into their careers or endeavors that meeting or securing the affections of a man is not a priority. Tragically, men, particularly black men, will use "The Word" as a masquerade to pursue black women sexually, financially, and emotionally. How needy the woman is dictates how fast she will fall for her pursuer's hidden agenda.

When some black women meet black men whom they perceive as "having it together," they open their hearts up (often without thorough considerations), and the contradictions begin. Some black men's game falls apart before any talk of marriage. Others keep their game together well into the marriage. Once the illusions of love subside, each party is able to make better assessments of each other's authentic character; but far too often, when this occurs it is too late. Not only does the marriage erode, but also the child's family lifestyle.

Dr. Erma Lawson, coauthor of *Black Men and Divorce* (1999), has done research that indicates the number one reason the fifty men in her study gave for divorcing their wives was money. The financial strain in these men's marriages seemed to outweigh all the other benefits of marriage, which included children. According to Lawson's research, the men found it difficult to maintain a middle-class status amid racial discrimination and social discrediting. In addition, the black men in Lawson's study felt that their ex-wives spent too much money on materialistic goods for their children. The men felt as though their authority as heads of their households was undermined; others were disgusted with their wives refusing what they considered better money management suggestions.

The other factors were social and political. The availability of black men is constantly narrowing due to drug addiction that leads to incarceration, suicide, and problems with the law. However, many black men feel that, since they are rare commodities, they should not have to work as hard to make a relationship or marriage work. Their rationale essentially becomes, if this relationship doesn't work, there are several other women waiting. In a *USA Today* article (March 7, 2000), marital therapist Audrey Chapman speaks in a similar vein: "Because available women so far outnumber them, many black men often say they see no reason to make long-term commitments." Both African American males and females in turn practice this philosophy at home or around extended kinships. In either case, temporary commitment practice becomes inbred in the psyche of African American youth.

Informing African American youth of divorce decisions appears to be the best choice, according to research. Authors Wallerstein and Kelly found that "children who were told that their fathers were planning to live elsewhere appeared less distraught than did those whose fathers disappeared without any explanations" (Wallerstein and Kelly, 1996, p. 188). Moreover, parents who give children forewarning of pending divorce decrease the chance of their child developing a negative perception of marriage.

According to Zinsmeister Karl (1996), the long-term effects of Divorce on children are: they're less imaginative; they become passive watchers; and they're more dependent, demanding, unaffectionate and disobedient than children from two parent (male & female) homes. Conversely, Amato & Sobolewski (2007) maintain that, "many children who experience divorce or grow up with discordant parents do not develop serious problems in adulthood", therefore some, but not all research may be exaggerated.

Since most experts agree that children suffer pain, guilt, and fear of abandonment when their parents divorce, these issues should be addressed. As painful as divorce is for the parents or caretakers, it's imperative that their children's pain is acknowledged. Communication with the children appears to be the best approach. Assuring them that they are neither at fault, nor are they the person who is being divorced, is necessary for their emotional well-being—especially for African American children, who often suffer indifference and rejection from the larger society.

CHAPTER 11

———◆◄———

Alternative Lifestyle

MOST HOMOSEXUAL AFRICAN AMERICANS REPORT THAT THEY KNEW they were gay at a fairly young age. They can vividly recall being attracted to the same sex; and adolescence is usually the age at which sexual experimentation begins. Youth who have no support—namely, from family members—as a result of their alternative sexuality can become suicidal; however, coping skills will vary for each individual.

During adolescence, African American males are under tremendous peer pressure to conform to an unwritten code that exemplifies down, cool, and hip. Adolescent gay males will date adolescent heterosexual females, regardless of their true feelings, in order to uphold the powerful unwritten code that young African American males hold close to their hearts. Author Jawanza Kunjufu echoes this same phenomenon by stating, "A boy and his peers will create their own definitions of manhood, especially when there is a physically or emotionally absent father" (Franklin, B.N., & Franklin, J.A. (2000), p. 144). He calls this the "code of the brotherhood." It is important to note that pressure to conform to the code of the brotherhood extends beyond the peers of gay African American youth. Both male and female members of the community participate in this activity as well. For example, note the following scenarios:

Scenario #1

CHRIS, A FIFTEEN-YEAR-OLD GAY JOCK, *has recently caught the attention of adult African American females. He's known in his community as the go-to guy on his basketball team. Like any other junior high or high school jock, Chris is pressured by his peers to prove his manhood. When Chris walks home from school, an adult black female makes a few flattering remarks to let Chris know that she is romantically interested. One particular remark points out features of Chris's manly body.*

Scenario #2

DWAYNE, A THIRTY-YEAR-OLD FACTORY WORKER, *has occasionally noticed how the neighborhood adult black females romantically respond to Chris. Like the lady in the first scenario, Dwayne does not know that Chris is gay.*

One day, Dwayne decides to pull Chris aside to inform him on his odds of engaging in sexual intercourse with an adult female in his neighborhood. Dwayne concludes this discussion with the remark, "Be a man." Given Chris's degree of orientation, he will respond to Dwayne's statement in one of two ways: the first response would be to actively initiate sex with those who are willing; the second unlikely response would be to find a rites-of-passage program. Odds are that Chris would be inclined to select the first response in order to uphold the brotherhood code.

Stereotypes

ALTHOUGH AFRICAN AMERICANS' ATTITUDES ABOUT gays and lesbians have improved, the stereotypes still exist. Authors such as Gary R. Howard (1999) suggest it is human nature to rank ourselves over one another. We humans possess a desire to feel superior to someone or something; however, of the homosexual stereotypes, many African Americans believe—and indirectly and directly pass on to their children—that all gay men are effeminate or all gay men are bad at sports. Anyone who has ever played organized sports in high school or college knows that this is false.

Clearly, the pressure for conformity can create havoc in the lives of gay male youth. This pressure to live up to someone else's definition of manhood causes gay males to suppress, deny, rationalize, and even question their genuine sexual orientation. For many black teenagers announcing that "I am gay," threatens their psychological well-being and could threaten their physical safety. Above all, this is a miniscule view of gay males' struggle to secure a position within family and community.

African American parents and immediate caregivers who discover that their son or daughter is gay usually have difficulty accepting it for two reasons: homophobia and religion. Whether or not parents or immediate caregivers come to terms with their child's sexual orientation varies with each parent.

Gay African American Males

THE AVERAGE AFRICAN AMERICAN RELIGION is Christianity, although a large number belong to Islam, and most black Christians and Muslims do not embrace homosexuality. In addition, homosexuality in the African American community is considered dishonorable. Where does this leave African American gay youth? How do they cope with this belief system? It is difficult living a lifestyle that is inconsistent with one's authentic self; thus many young people are hesitant to expose their sexuality, especially African American males. They maintain the façade of being heterosexual until they're no longer able to. After countless years of deception runs its course, devising a plan to confide in the family becomes the alternative, risking rejection and ridicule from people closest to them. For a gay black male, confiding in a family member—coming out of the closet—serves as baby steps.

When African American parents become aware that their son is gay, many panic, become angry, or fall into a state of denial. The following scenario will serve as an example of a typical reaction of the average religious African American parent to their son's coming-out.

Scenario #3

HENRY IS A SIXTEEN-YEAR-OLD HONOR student who loves to play the piano. Mary, Henry's mother, has noticed several articles dealing with homosexuality in his room. Henry, being an honor student, leads Mary to believe that the

139

articles were just for a school report. She was also suspicious of Henry's less-than-masculine appearance. One day, Henry decided to come out. He decided to inform his mother before he informed his friends about his sexual orientation. His mother couldn't handle it; she called him a "sinner" and told him, "God will punish you, and you will go to hell." Henry was deeply hurt. As harsh and crass as Henry's mother's response was, it is a typical reaction for a parent.

Gay African American Females

ANNOUNCING ONE'S SEXUALITY AS A gay female adolescent creates a unique set of challenges as well. Like the male, the female has to bear hostile societal pressure, feelings of alienation, invisibility, and parents and immediate caregivers who may or may not accept their child's sexual orientation. The female youth, like the male youth, must contend with a chronically homophobic community. This reality creates more alienation and fear about disclosing her sexual interest in women.

Black adolescent females who have undergone this experience often have voiced their reluctance to confide even in their closest peers about their alternative lifestyle. This silence is primarily due to fear of stigma or labeling in the community. As mentioned in several recent publications for African Americans, unlike for many other ethnic groups, homophobia is ingrained in their religion, which serves as a legitimate justification of the widespread notion. However, according to recent research, once black adolescent females decide to come out, their parents normally accept them, but sometimes on the condition that they keep their child's lesbianism a family secret. Sometimes, the mother will decide to put her ambiguous feelings aside and love her child. Often, the siblings' feelings are ambivalent.

Parents and caretakers cannot determine their daughter's sexual preference by her associates or clothing. Likewise, feminist and women's movement magazines in a young female's possession are not indicators that she is a homosexual, but it is a possible sign of homosexual experimentation.

Moreover, black lesbian adolescents lack role models who are homosexual, which is also true for black gay male adolescents. This void makes it even more difficult to form a positive alternative identity as an adolescent. Similar to heterosexual black youth, young lesbians also need someone in their lives or in the media that looks like them and resonates similar values and positive behaviors. The confusion that most African American adolescents experience can only be clarified and felt by someone who has undergone a similar experience. Growing up in America black and lesbian leaves many young women feeling abnormal, especially when they find themselves attracted to other females—sometimes close friends. Because it is expected of them, many young lesbians date heterosexual males but find no genuine attraction to or interest in them.

Alternative lifestyles of the homosexual African American youth require the same respect as all other aspects of the developing experience. Once again, education is the key, which must begin with the family unit, then the community—the churches and schools. Tolerance is the underlying element that needs to be stressed, hopefully to be followed by acceptance.

CONCLUSION

—▶ ◀—

POSITIVE SOCIALIZATION OF THE AFRICAN American child, no matter how one views it, involves a community effort. No parent or immediate caregiver can do it all. An interaction of other positive people is needed along with an extended support system. Parents and immediate caregivers tend to do their children better service with outside input while navigating them through childhood and adolescence.

One of the greatest mistakes parents make with their children is doing too much for them. The goal is to raise children for autonomy; instead, parents will rationalize their overindulgence by professing that they don't want their children to have to struggle as they did. Giving children everything that they didn't have could cripple them. It may hinder their ability to become independent, self-reliant, and productive adults.

I reiterate listen to your children. A good rapport with them will warrant not only discussions of their fears and disappointments, but also good and bad encounters with other adults in their lives, whether they're teachers, preachers, grocers or UPS service persons or even other youngsters. To be able to always confide in you helps shape their sense of worthiness.

Lastly, hold the African American youth accountable for their own peace of mind, happiness and successes with their endeavors. They must be made to understand they are as important to—as responsible for their successes and/or failures as the various institutions, i.e., the family, the community, the school, the church and the work place.

As aforementioned, there are no blueprints in life, only sketches or structure or improvisation. Although divided, African Americans need to collectively decide if the culture is worth preserving. Currently, it is in a state of emergency. African American youth need to be socialized to properly handle the setbacks and challenges that lie ahead for them in America and the world.

RESOURCES

Interracial Family Organizations

Contact AMEA for group near you. Here is a sampling from around the nation.

Biracial Family Network

P.O. Box 3214

Chicago, IL 60654

Interracial Families in Friendship
P.O. Box 82628
Columbus, OH 43202

http://www.insouciant.com/ifif/resource.htm

E-mail janet@simplyliving.org or wolftale@wolftale.net

Financial Resource Organizations

Association of Black Women Entrepreneurs

P.O. Box 49368

Los Angeles, CA 90049

(213) 624-8369

National Association of Black Women Entrepreneurs (NABWE)

P.O. Box 1375

Detroit, MI 48231

(810) 356-3686

Fax (810) 354-3793

Minority Business Entrepreneur (MBE)

3528 Torrance Boulevard, Suite 101

Torrance, CA 90503-4803

(310) 540-9398

Fax (310) 792-8263

E-mail mbewbe@ix.netcom.com

Web site: www.mbemag.com

Jump $tart Coalition

for Personal Financial Literacy

919 18th St., NW, 3rd Floor

Washington, DC 20006

888-45-EDUCATE

Web site: www.jumpstartcoalition.org

Articles

"All Mixed Up"

www.salon.com/news/feature/2000/02/14/mixed_race/index.html

Salon.com features a series of articles on America's multiracial future.

"Blurring the Lines"

www.washington.edu/alumni/columns/dec96

Maria P.P. Root, a clinical psychologist who has edited groundbreaking books on the multiracial experience, is featured.

"Is That Your Child? Mothers Talk about Rearing Biracial Children"

http://thedefendersonline.com/2009/03/23/is-that-your-child-mothers-talk-about-rearing-biracial-children/

This article explores unique experiences of black and white mothers of biracial children.

Family Planning

Planned Parenthood

810 Seventh Avenue

New York, NY 10019

(212) 603-4600

National Black Women's Health Project
1237 Abernathy SW
Atlanta, GA 30310
(404) 758-9590

Women's Health Network
1325 G Street NW
Washington, DC 20005
(202) 347-1140

The National Foundation for Teaching Entrepreneurship
(NFTE)
120 Wall Street, 29th floor
New York, NY 10005
(800) FOR-NFTE
http://www.nfte.com

National Association for Equal Opportunity in Higher Education
8701 Georgia Avenue, Suite 200
Silver Spring, MD 20910
(301) 650-2440
http://www.nafeo.org

United Negro College Fund
8260 Willow Oaks Corporate Drive
Fairfax, VA 22031
(800) 331-2244
http://www.uncf.org

Black Excel: The College Help Network
PMB H281
New York, NY 10001
(212) 591-1936

U.S. Department of Education
400 Maryland Avenue, SW
Washington, DC 20202
(800) USA-LEARN or (800) 872-5327
http://www.ed.gov

The Student Center
http://www.student.com/

Educational On-Line Listing of Historically Black Colleges and Universities
http://www.edonline.com/cq/hbcu

U.S. Department of Education
http://www.ed.gov/index.jhtml

Federal Student Aid Information Center
(800) 4-FED-AID or (800) 433-3243
http://www.fafsa.ed.gov

Girls' Pipeline to Power
95 Berkeley Street
Boston, MA 02116
(617) 482-1078
http://www.girlspipeline.org

Association for Women in Computing
41 Sutter Street, Suite 1006
San Francisco, CA 94104
(415) 905-4663
http://www.awc-hq.org

Sexuality

Gay and Lesbian Youth Advocacy Council
55 Mason Street
San Francisco, CA 94102

National Gay Youth Network
P.O. Box 846
San Francisco, CA 94101

National Lesbian and Gay Health Foundation
1638 R Street, NW, Suite 2
Washington, DC 20009

National Youth Advocacy Coalition
1711 Connecticut Avenue, NW, Suite 206
Washington, DC 20009-1139

PFLAG (Parents, Families and Friends of Lesbians and Gays)
11012 14th Street, NW, #700
Washington, DC 20005
www.pflag.org

Alyson Publications, Inc.
www.alyson.com
Books for gay teens and others on political, legal, financial, medical, spiritual, social, and sexual issues

Canadian Gay, Lesbian & Bisexual Resource
Directory
www.gaycanada.com
Canada's community-based gay, lesbian, and bisexual information network

GLBT National Hotline

www.glnh.org

Describes services available and links to other gay and lesbian hotlines

!OutProud!

www.outproud.org

Wide range of resources from the National Coalition for Gay, Lesbian, Bisexual and Transgender Youth

National Runaway Hotline

1 (800) 621-4000

TDD: 1 (800) 621-0394

National Teen HIV/AIDS Hotline

(Fridays and Saturdays 6 PM.–12 AM Eastern Time)

1 (800) 440-TEEN (8336)

National STD Hot Line

1 (800) 227-8922

Couples' Therapists

Prep, Inc.

1780 S. Bellaire St., Suite 621

Denver, CO 80222

American Association of Marriage and Family Therapists

1100 17th St., NW, 10th Floor

Washington, DC 20136

Black Family Organizations

Freedom Institute

515 Madison Avenue

New York, NY 10017

(212) 838-0044

Books can be ordered through them.

Dollars & Sense for College Students by Ellen Briatman (Random House/ Princeton Review, 1998); $11.

Get a Financial Life: Personal

Children's Defense Fund
25 E Street, NW
Washington, DC 20001
(202) 628-8787
www.childrensdefense.org
E-mail: cdfinfo@childrensdefense.org

Advocacy/Help for Survivors

Rape, Abuse & Incest National Network
635B Pennsylvania Avenue, SE
Washington, DC 20003
(202) 544-1034, ext. 1
(800) 656-HOPE; (800) 656-4673
www.rainn.org

Black Women's Health Imperative
www.blackwomenshealth.org

National Organization for Women
(202) 331-9002
733 15th Street, NW, 2nd Floor
Washington, DC 20005
www.now.org

Men Can Stop Rape
PO Box 57144
Washington, DC 20037
(202) 265-6530
www.mencanstoprape.org

Rosa Parks Sexual Assault Crisis Center

4182 S. Western Avenue

Los Angeles, CA 90062

(223) 290-4119

V-Day

http://www.vday.org

The National Center for Victims of Crime

2000 M Street, NW, Suite 480

Washington, DC 20036

(202) 467-8700

(800) FYI-CALL; (800) 349-2255

www.ncvc.org

Religion-Based Support

SASSY, Inc.

PO Box 727

Rice Lake, WI 54868

(715) 234-8445

www.sassyinc.org

Help for Men

Male Survivor: The National Organization Against Male Sexual Victimization

PMB 103

5505 Connecticut Avenue, NW

Washington, DC 20015

(800) 738-4181

www.malesurvivor.org

Juvenile Justice Organizations

Coalition for Juvenile Justice
2030 M St., NW, Suite 701
Washington, DC 20036
(202) 467-0864
juvjustice.org

Juvenile Justice Educational Enhancement Program
345 S. Magnolia Drive, Suite D-23
Tallahassee, FL 32301-2987
(850) 414-8355
http://www.fldoe.org/ese/dr-jjeep.asp

National Center for Juvenile Justice
710 Fifth Ave.
Pittsburgh, PA 15219-3000
(412) 227-6950
http://www.ncjjservehttp.org/NCJJWebsite/main.html

Religious Organizations

The African Methodist Episcopal Church
http://www.ame-church.com/directory/

The African Methodist Episcopal Zion Church
http://www.amez.org/news/amezion/aboutourchurch.html

The Christian Methodist Episcopal Church
www.cmesonline.org

The Nation of Islam
www.finalcall.com

People for the American Way
African American Religious Affairs
2000 M Street NW, Suite 400
Washington, D.C. 20036
202-467-4999
http://site.pfaw.org/site/PageServer?pagename=leadership_aara

These sites provide general history of African American religious life.
Black and Christian
www.blackandchristian.com

Black History (*Encyclopedia Britannica*)
http://www.britannica.com/blackhistory

The Internet Public Library
http://www.ipl.org/div/subject/browse/soc40.05.00/

PBS: Africa
www.pbs.org/wnet/africa/

APPENDIX 1-A: CULTURAL FACTORS THAT CONTRIBUTE TO CHILDHOOD OBESITY.

—▶ ◀—

NOTED BELOW ARE SEVERAL CULTURAL factors that contribute to the child obesity epidemic:

- The sedentary effect of TV, the Internet, and video games—running around the neighborhood and playing outside is a thing of the past

- 70 percent of our kids spend two hours per day with some kind of "screen media"

- Mandatory PE hours cut from school curriculums

- Kids rarely walking or riding bikes—almost half of all children do not participate in *any* physical activity.

- Safety concerns to keep kids indoors

- Soft drinks and junk foods—consuming "empty calories" rather than balanced meals

- Vending machine offerings available throughout the day

- Soft drinks—an especially bad health "bargain" (costing the least to upsize, delivering the biggest calorie boost, and giving retailers some of the highest profit margins)

  Studies show a one-quarter pound gain per week in kids drinking more than twelve-ounce soda per day

- Eating more calories per bite—through processed foods with added sugar and added fat

- Super-sized portions—our consumption-driven culture of abundance and entitlement
- "Value marketing"—encourages overeating (we feel compelled to consume our entire purchase)
- Market-driven cultural changes—greater use of prepared foods and frequent eating out

Source: Reprint of Oklahoma Fit Kids Coalition

BIBLIOGRAPHY

Akers, C. (2000). *Obesity.* San Diego, CA: Lucent Books, Inc.

Atwater, E. (1996) *Adolescence* (4th ed.). Upper Saddle River, NJ: Prentice Hall.

Bailey, W.A., and Hale, J.E. (2000). *Learning While Black: Creating Educational Excellence for African American Children.* Baltimore, MD: The Johns Hopkins University Press

Banks, I. (2000) *Hair Matters: Beauty, Power, and Black Women's Consciousness.* New York, NY: New York University Press.

Barnard, N. Lanou, A. and Physicians Committee for Responsible Medicine. (2002). *Healthy Eating for Life for Children.* New York, NY: John Wiley & Sons, Inc.

Bennett, L. (2007) *Before the Mayflower: A History of Black America.* Chicago, IL: Johnson Publishing Company, Inc.

Billingsley, A. (1999) *Mighty Like a River: The Black Church and Social Reform.* New York, NY: Oxford University Press.

Blumberg, S.L., Markman, H.J., Stanley, S.M., and Whitfield, K.E. (2001). *Fighting for Your African American Marriage.* San Francisco, CA: Jossey-Bass.

Boston, E. K. (1996). *Smart Money For African Americans.* New York, NY: G.P. Putnam's Sons.

Boyd, A. J. (1993). *In The Company of My Sisters: Black Women and Self-Esteem.* New York, NY: Penguin Group.

Boykin, Keith. (1996) *One More River to Cross: Black and Gay in America*. New York, NY: Doubleday.

Brown, Liz, and Challem, Jack (2002) *Basic Health Publications User's Guide to Vitamins & Minerals*. North Bergen, NJ: Basic Health Publications, Inc.

Brown, M. Ursula (2001) *The Interracial Experience: Growing Up Black/White Racially Mixed in the United States*. Westport, CT: Praeger Publishers.

Brown, Tony (1998) *Empower the People: Overthrow the Conspiracy That Is Stealing Your Money and Freedom*. New York, NY: William Morrow and Company, Inc.

Butts, H.F., and Haskins, J. (1993) The *Psychology of Black Language*. New York, NY: Hippocrene Books.

Carrasquillo, A.L. (2002). *Language Minority Students in the Mainstream Classroom*. Philadelphia, PA: Multilingual Matters Ltd.

Chatters, L.M., Jackson, J.S., and Taylor R.J. (1997) *Family Life in Black America*. Thousand Oaks, CA: Sage Publications.

Coates, B.A. (1999). *Divorce with Decency: The Complete How-to Handbook and Survivor's Guide to the Legal, Emotional, Economic, and Social Issues*. Honolulu, HI: University of Hawaii Press.

Cose, E. (1993). *The Rage of a Privileged Class*. New York, NY: Harper Collins Publishers.

Cox, R. Melissa, and Reisser, C. Paul, MD (2002) *Teen Health: Raising Physically and Emotionally Healthy Teens*. Wheaton, IL: Tyndale House Publications, Inc.

Crohn, J. (1995). *Mixed Matches: How to Create Successful Interracial, Interethnic, and Interfaith Relationships*. New York, NY: Fawcett Columbine-Ballantine Books.

Cromsky, N. (1994) *Secrets, Lies and Democracy*. Tucson, AZ: Odonian Press.

DeBose, C.E., Keulen, J.E., and Weddington, G.T. (1997). *Speech,*

Language, Learning, and the African American Child. Boston, MA: Allyn and Bacon.

Dixon, M. B. & Wilson, J. (1994) *Good Health for African Americans.* New York, NY: Crown Publishers, Inc.

Dobson, E. G., Feinberg, C.L, Hindson, E. E., Kroll, W. M., Willmington, H. L. (1994) *The KJV Parallel Bible Commentary.* Atlanta, GA: Thomas Nelson Publishers.

Dowd, E. Merle (1994) *Money, Banking, and Credit Made Simple.* New York, NY: Doubleday.

Dyer, W.W. (2001). *There's a Spiritual Solution to Every Problem.* New York, NY: Harper Collins Publishers, Inc.

Endersbe, K. Julie (2000). *Homosexuality: What Does It Mean?* Mankato, MN: Capstone Press.

Evans, I.R. (1989). *Albert Bandura: the man and his ideas-a dialogue.* New York, NY: Praeger Publishers, A division of Greenwood Press, Inc.

Fallar, K. (2003) *Understanding and Assessing Child Sexual Maltreatment.* Thousand Oaks, CA: Sage Publications, Inc.

Fisher, M.P. (1999). *Religion in the Twenty-First Century.* Upper Saddle River, NJ: Prentice Hall.

Ford, C.A., and Lang, M. (1988). *Black Student Retention in Higher Education.* Springfield, IL: Charles C. Thomas.

Ford, T. Michael (1998). *Outspoken: Role Models from the Lesbian and Gay Community.* New York, NY: Morrow Junior Books.

Francis, H. (1999). *Church Planting: In the African American Context.* Grand Rapids, MI: Zondervan Publishing House.

Franklin B. Nancy, Franklin, A.J., and Toussaint A. Pamela (2000) *Boys into Men: Raising Our African American Teenage Sons.* New York, NY: Penguin Group.

Frazier, Sundee T. (2002). *Check All That Apply: Finding Wholeness as a Multiracial Person.* Downers Grove, IL: InterVarsity Press.

Free, M. (1995). *African Americans and the Criminal Justice System*. New York, NY: Garland Publishing, Inc.

Fukuyama, Francis (1996). *Trust: The Social Virtues and the Creation of Prosperity*. New York. NY: The Free Press.

Gail, L. Thompson (2004). *Through Ebony Eyes: What Teachers Need to Know But Are Afraid to Ask about African American Students*. San Francisco, CA: John Wiley & Sons, Inc.

Gleason, J.B. (2000). *The Development of Language*. Boston, MA: Allyn & Bacon.

Goldberg, C. Albert (2000). *Feed Your Child Right from Birth through Teens*. New York, NY: M. Evans and Company, Inc.

Gooden, S. Kumea, and Jones, Charisse (2003). *Shifting: The Double Lives of Black Women in America*. New York, NY: HarperCollins Publishers Inc.

Gordon, Judith, and Gordon, Sol (2000). *Raising a Child Responsibly in a Sexually Permissive World*. Holbrook, MA: Adams Media Corporation.

Haight, W.L. (2002). *African American Children at Church: A Sociocultural Perspective*. New York, NY: Cambridge University Press.

Hale, J.E. (1986). *Black Children: Their Roots, Culture, and Learning Styles*. Baltimore, MD: The Johns Hopkins University Press

Hardin, N. Kimeron (1999). *The Gay and Lesbian Self-Esteem Book: A Guide to Loving Ourselves*. Oakland, CA: New Harbinger Publications, Inc.

Harris, Fran (1998). *In the Black: The African-American Parent's Guide to Raising Financially Responsible Children*. New York, NY: Fireside.

Hatherington, E.M., and Parke, R.D. (1993). *Child Psychology: A Contemporary Viewpoint* (4th ed.) San Francisco, CA: McGraw-Hill, Inc.

Healey, J.F. (1995*). Race, Ethnicity, Gender, and Class: The Sociology of Group Conflict and Change*. Thousand Oaks, CA: Pine Forge Press.

Hill, S.A. (1999). *African American Children: Socialization and Development in Families.* Thousand Oaks, CA: Sage Publications.

Hooks, B. (2005). *Sisters of the yam: black women and self-recovery.* Cambridge, MA: South End Press.

Howard, R. G. (1999). *We Can't Teach What We Don't Know: White Teachers, Multiracial Schools.* New York, NY: Teachers College Press.

Huff, A., and Mills, R. (1999). *Style over Substance: A Critical Analysis of an African American Teenage Subculture.* Chicago, IL: African American Images.

Johnson, B. Leanor, and Staples, Robert (1993). *Black Families at the Crossroads: Challenges and Prospects.* San Francisco, CA: Jossey-Bass Publishers.

Johnson, David (1997). *Minorities and Girls in School: Effects on Achievement and Performance.* Thousand Oaks, CA: Sage Publications.

Jones, A. Paul, and Mitchell, Angela (2000). *Heart Disease and Hypertension: Vital Health Information for African Americans.* New York, NY: Kensington Publishing Corp.

Kunjufu, J. (1997). *Adam! Where Are You?: Why Most Black Men Don't Go to Church.* Sauk Villiage, IL: African American Images.

Lawson, J. Erma, and Thompson, Aaron (1999). *Black Men and Divorce.* Thousand Oaks, CA: Sage Publications, Inc.

Lee, C.C. (1996). *Saving the Native Son: Empowerment Strategies for Young Black Males.* Greensboro, NC: ERIC/CASS Publications.

Lincoln, E.C., and Lawrence, M.H. (1990). *The Black Church in the African American Experience.* Durham, NC: Duke University Press.

Logan, L.M. Sadye (2001). *The Black Family: Strengths, Self-Help, and Positive Change.* Boulder, CO: Westview Press, Inc.

Lundin, W.R, (1991). *Theories and Systems of Psychology* (4th ed.) Lexington, MA: D.C. Health and Company.

Major, C., (1994). *Juba to Jive: A Dictionary of African-American Slang.* Puffin Books.

Matthew, K., and Pratt, S.G. (2006).*SuperFoods HealthStyle: Simple Changes to Get the Most Out of Life for the Rest of Your Life.* New York, NY: Harper Collins Publishers

McAdoo, H.P. (2002*). Black Children* (2ⁿᵈ ed.) Thousand Oaks, CA: Sage Publications, Inc.

McCarthy, R. Alice (1997). *Healthy Teens: Success in High School* (2ⁿᵈ ed.) Birmingham, MI: Bridge Communications, Inc.

Jackson, Jesse L., Jr. (1999). *It's About The Money!* New York, NY: Three River Press.

McMickle, A. Marvin (2000). *Preaching to the Black Middle Class.* Valley Forge, PA: /Judson Press.

Miller, M.B. (2002). *How to Get Rich When You Ain't Got Nothing: The African American Guide to Gaining and Building Wealth.* Phoenix, AZ: Amber Books.

Murphy, L. (2000). *Down by the Riverside: Readings in African American Religion (Religion, Race, and Ethnicity)* New York, NY: NYU Press.

Murphy, G. L. (2003). *African American Faith in America.* New York, NY: Facts On File, Inc.

Nichter, Mimi (2000). *Fat Talk: What Girls and Their Parents Say about Dieting.* Cambridge,   MA: Harvard University Press.

Ogbu, U. John (2003). *Black American Students in an Affluent Suburb: A Study of Academic Disengagement.* Mahwah, NJ: Lawrence Erlbaum Associates, Inc., Publishers.

O'Hearn, C. Claudine (1998). *Half and Half: Writers on Growing Up Biracial and Bicultural.* New York, NY: Pantheon Books.

Perryman, W. (2003). *Unfounded Loyalty.* Lanham, MD: PNEUMA Life Publishing.

Phoenix, Ann, and Tizard, Barbara (1993). *Black, White or Mixed Race?: Race and Racism in the Lives of Young People of Mixed Parenting.* New York, NY: Routledge Publishing.

Physicians Committee for Responsible Medicine (2002) *Healthy Eating for Life for Children*. New York, NY: Wiley.

Piaget, J. (2001). *The Language And Thought Of The Child*. New York, NY: Routledge Publishing

Porterfield, K.M. (1981). *Straight Talk About Divorce*. New York, NY: Facts On File Publishing.

Reuter, E.B. (2007). *The Mulatto In The United States: Including A Study Of The Role Of Mixed-Blood Races Throughout The World*. Whitefish, MT: Kessinger Publishing, LLC

Rickford R. John, and Rickford, J. Russell (2000). *Spoken Soul: The Story of Black English*. Danvers, MA: John Wiley & Sons, Inc.

Rifkin, I. (2003). *Spiritual Perspectives on Globalization: Making Sense of Economic and Cultural Upheaval*. Woodstock, VT: Skylight Paths Publishing.

Sher, Brian (2000). *What Rich People Know and Desperately Want to Keep Secret*. Roseville, CA: PRIMA SOHO.

Sobel, M. (1979). *Trabelin' On: The Slave Journey to an Afro-Baptist Faith*. Princeton, NJ: Princeton University Press.

Stephens, Brooke M. (1999). *Wealth Happens One Day at a Time*. New York, NY: HarperCollins Publishers, Inc.

Stephens, Brooke (1997). *Talking Dollars and Making Sense: Wealth-Building Guide for African Americans*. New York. NY: McGraw-Hill.

Sherman, R.J. (1992). *African-American Poetry of the Nineteenth Century: AN ANTHOLOGY*. Champaign, IL: University of Illinois Press.

Stone, R. (2004). *No Secrets, No Lies: How Black Families Can Heal from Sexual Abuse*. New York, NY: Broadway Books.

Tatum, B.D. (1997). *Why Are All the Black Kids Sitting Together in the Cafeteria?* New York, NY: Basic Books.

Thernstrom, A., and Thernstrom, S. (2003). *No Excuses: Closing the Racial Gap in Learning*. New York, NY: Simon & Schuster.

Tyson, A. (2001). *How I Retired at 26: A Step-by-Step Guide to Accessing Your Freedom and Wealth at Any Age.* ATD Publishing

U.S. Census Bureau (2000) *Population of the United States by Race and Hispanic Origin: 2000 Census Results.* Washington, DC: Government Printing Office.

Valade, R. M. III (1996). *Black Literature Guide.* .Detroit, MI: Visible Ink Press.

Villarosa, L. (1994). *The Black Women's Guide to Physical Health and Emotional Well- Being.* New York, NY: Harper Perennial.

Wallerstein, J.S., and Kelly, J.B. (1996). *The Breakup: How Children and Parents Cope With Divorce.* New York, NY: Basic Books.

Ward, V. Janie (2000). *The Skin We're In: Teaching Our Children to Be Emotional.* New York, NY: The Free Press.

Warneryd, K.E. (1999). *The Psychology of Saving: A Study on Economic Psychology.* Northampton, MA: Edward Elgar Publishing.

West, C. (1994). *Race Matters.* New York, NY: Vintage Books.

Woodson, C.G. (1990). *The Mis-Education of The Negro.* Trenton, NJ: Africa World Press, Inc.

Wolman, R.N. (2001). *Thinking with Your Soul: Spiritual Intelligence and Why It Matters.* New York, NY: Harmony Books.

Wright, A. Marguerite (1998). *I'm Chocolate, You're Vanilla: Raising Healthy Black and Biracial Children in a Race-Conscious World.* San Francisco, CA: Jossey-Bass Inc.

Magazine Articles

Bennett, A., Chatzky, J.S., Daragahi, B., Feldman, A., Feldman, J., Geary, L.H., Kirwan, R., Wang, P., and Weisser, C. (2001, September) "Family Matters." *Money*, pp. 74–96.

Bush, V. (2002, September). "The War on Girls: Fat Chances." *Essence*, pp. 76–80.

Caviness, G.Y. (2002, April) "But Mommy, White Dolls Are Prettier: Teaching Your Daughter to Embrace Her Own Beauty." *Essence*, pp. 124–126, 148.

Caviness, G.Y. (2002, September) "Homeschooling Rules." *Essence*, pp. 214–216.

Davis, K. (2002, August) "How to Raise a Genius (or at Least a B-Plus Student)." *Ebony*, pp. 110–114.

English, T.R. (2006, Dec) "Saving Black boys: is single-sex education the answer?" *Ebony*, pp.52-55.

Gravin, J.R. (2002, July) "Diabetes: Simple Steps Can Cut the Risk of Acquiring the Mysterious Disease." *Jet*, p 20.

Jeffers, G. (2001, August). "How to Raise Black Boys." *Ebony*, p.58.

Lamb, Y.R., and Scruggs, A.O. (2002) "The War on Girls: Talking to Our Girls About Sex." *Essence,* pp. 142–144.

Linden, E. (1991, September). "Lost Tribes—Lost Knowledge." *Time*, p. 24.

Marcus, D.A. (2001, August) "The Gospel of Money." *Money*, pp. 99–103.

Mary, L. (2003, August) "Freedom of Choice." *Essence,* pp. 178–188.

Moore, T. (2001, August/September) "Investing 101: Ways of Making Your Money Count." *Black Diaspora*, p. 54.

Morgan, J. (2002, June) Sex, Lies and Videos. *Essence*, pp. 120–124.

Semple, B.O. (2001, October) "Diabetes: A Growing Concern among Blacks." *Black Diaspora*, pp. 41–42.

Villarosa, L. (2002, January) "Our Girls in Crisis." *Essence.* pp. 92–95.

Whitaker, C. (2001, April) "Why Are Young Black Men Killing Themselves?" *Ebony*, pp. 144–146.

Internet Sites

Centers for Disease Control and Prevention (CDC), Nutrition for

Everyone (2005). Retrieved June 15, 2009 from http://www.cdc.gov/nutrition/everyone/basics/fat/index.html

National Center for Health Statistics, Teen Birth Rate Continues to Decline; African-American Teens Show Sharpest Drop (2002). Retrieved October 6, 2009 from http://www.cdc.gov/nchs/PRESSROOM/03facts/teenbirth.htm

Jacobson. F. M., (July 13, 2005) "Press Conference on Soft Drinks" Retrieved May 18, 2009 from http://cspinet.org/new/pdf/final_mfj_soda_statement.pdf

Gang. C.A., (September 5, 2004) "Martial arts can be prescription for self-confidence" Retrieved May 24, 2009 http://www2.ljworld.com/news/2004/sep/05/martial_arts_can/?print

Table 1. Deaths and percentage of deaths for the 10 leading causes of death: United States, 2002 – 2003. Retrieved June 16, 2009 from http://www.cdc.gov/nchs/data/hestat/leadingdeaths03_tables.pdf#1

The News Media's Picture of Children: A Five-Year Update and A Focus on Diversity – 1999 Retrieved May 14, 2009 from http://publications.childrennow.org/publications/media/newsmedia_1999b.cfm

Boulware. C., (1998-2006) "Adult Survivors of Childhood Sexual Abuse" Retrieved October 26, 2009 from http://www.psychotherapist.net/adultsurvivors.html

The National Institute of Health: Sexual Transmitted Diseases

Retrieved October 26, 2009 from http://www.nichd.nih.gov/health/topics/sexually_transmitted_diseases.cfm

Beacham, S., "Money Savvy Generation" Retrieved November 12, 2009 from http://www.msgen.com/assembled/money_savvy_pig.html

Ellison, S.M., (2000, August) "Anorexia and Women of Color." Retrieved July 7, 2003, from http://www.suite101.com/article.cfm/anorexia/45443

"Adolescent Nutrition: A Neglected Dimension." Retrieved May

20, 2009, from http://www.who.int/mip2001/files/2233/ NHDbrochurecentrefold.pdf

Socialization (January 3, 2009) Retrieved May 14, 2009 from http:// anthro.palomar.edu/social/soc_1.htm

Russell, M. R. & Suter, M. P. (2001). Good Health to Diet For: Blood Pressure and Nutrition. Retrieved May 18, 2009 from http:// thedoctorwillseeyounow.com/articles/nutrition/bpsalt_13/

Keane, S. (1997) "Questioning Socialization." Retrieved July 23, 2004, from http://mypage.direct.ca/s/skeane/socializ.html

Reisser, C.P., (1993) "Sex and Singles: Reasons to Wait." Retrieved May 26, 2009, from http://www.allbabiescherished.com/abstinence. htm

"Extracurricular Activities" (Undated) Retrieved July 13, 2004, from http://kidshealth.org/teen/school_jobs/school/involved_school. html

"Jumpstart Coalition for Personal Financial Literacy." Retrieved November 20, 2009, from http://www.jumpstartcoalition.org/

What's up wif Ebonics, Y'all? (Undated). Retrieved June 22, 2002, from http://www.readingonline.org/articles/gupta/ebonics.html

Selfhelp Magazine
http://www.selfhelpmagazine.com/articles/eating/nih/common. html

"Eating Disorders." Retrieved May 20, 2009, from http://mentalhealth. samhsa.gov/publications/allpubs/ken98-0047/default.asp

"Eating Disorders Warning Signs." Retrieved July 7, 2003, from Kid Source Online Web site http://www.kidsource.com/nedo/ warning.html

"Understanding Lactose Intolerance." Retrieved September 9, 2003, from http://lactoseintolerant.org/02_about.html

Centers for Disease Control and Prevention (CDC), Leading Causes of Death in Males United States, (2004). Retrieved May 25, 2009, from http://www.cdc.gov/men/lcod/index.htm

World Health Organization (WHO), "Cancer." February 2009, from http://www.who.int/mediacentre/factsheets/fs297/en/index.html

Peterson, K.S. (2000, March) "Black Couples Stay the Course." *USA Today*. Retrieved September 22, 2003, from http://www.divorcereform.org/mel/rdivorceblack.html

Taylor A.C. (1998, June) " Perceptions of Intergenerational Bonds: The Comparison Between Grandfathers and their Adult Grandchildren." Retrieved November 3, 2009 from http://scholar.lib.vt.edu/theses/available/etd-6898-214743/unrestricted/etd.PDF

Kolsti, N.(1999). "African-American Men Suffer after Divorce, Study Finds." *News Service*. Retrieved May 11, 2009, from University of North Texas Web site: http://web3.unt.edu/news/story.cfm?story=7459

Sahgal, N. & Smith, G. (2009, January) "A Religious Portrait of African-Americans." *The Pew Forum on Religion & Public Life*. Retrieved May 28, 2009, from http://pewforum.org/docs/?DocID=389

West, A. & Besharov, J.D. (2000, August) " African American Marriage Patterns" *Hoover Press: Thernstorm*. Retrieve September 20, 2001, from http://www.welfareacademy.org/pubs/family/africanamericanmarriage.pdf

Periodical Article

Wiley, E. (1990) "Cool Posing: Misinterpreted Expressions Often Lead to Educational Deprivation." *Black Issues in Higher Education*, Sept. pp. 6–7.

Journal Articles

Amato, R. P. & Sobolewski, M. J. (2007) "Parents' Discord & Divorce, Parent – Child Relationships and Subjective Well-Being in Early Adulthood: Is Feeling Close to

Two Parents Always Better than Feeling Close to One? *Social Forces. Chapel Hill,* v85, p1105(20). Retrieved July 12, 2009 from ProQuest database.

Anonymous (2003) "Mentors are Key to Getting Black Students to College, Study Says." *Black Issues in Higher Education,* 20: 20–21. Retrieved June 13, 2003, from ProQuest database.

Berry, G.L. (1998) "Black Family Life on Television and the Socialization of the African American Child: Images of Marginality." *Journal of Comparative Family Studies,* 29: 233–242. Retrieved October 12, 2002, from ProQuest database.

Birman, D. (1984) "Biculturalism and Ethnic Identity: An Integrated Model." *The Society for the Psychological Study of Ethnic Minority Issues,* 8: 9–11.

Byers, K.G. & Savaiano, D.A. (2005) "The Myth of Increased Lactose Intolerance in African-Americans." *Journal of the American College of Nutrition,* v24(6). Retrieved May 28, 2009, from Medline Detailed Record database.

Flowers, C., Garrett, M.T., McMillan, S.N., Roberts, E.M. (2006) " Ebony and Ivory: Relationship Between African American Young Women's Skin Color and Ratings of Self and Peers." *Journal of Humanistic Counseling, Education and Development,* v45, p79(16). Retrieved June 18, 2009 from ProQuest database.

Hale, R.P. (1996) "Reflections on the Importance of Role Models: An African American Teacher Defends Use of Black Role Models." *Black Issues in Higher Education,* v13, p22(2). Retrieved July 31, 2000, from Infotrac database.

Hall, A.P. (1997) "The Ebonics debate: Are we speaking the same language? *The Black Scholar,* v27, p12(3). Retrieved June 23, 2009, from ProQuest database.

Hepburn, M.A. (1998) "The Power of the Electronic Media in the Socialization of Young Americans: Implications for Social Studies Education." *The Social Studies,* 89: 71. Retrieved June 18, 1999 from Infotrac database.

Hill, S.A. (2001) "Class, Race, and Gender Dimensions of Child Rearing in African American Families." *Journal of Black Studies*, 31: 494–508.

Hope, C. (2002) "Trends in Global Obesity." *The Futurist*, 36: 10. Retrieved April 4, 2005, from ProQuest database.

Kaplan, E.B. (2000) "African American Children: Socialization and Development in Families." *Contemporary Sociology*, 29: 825–826. Retrieved October 12, 2002, from ProQuest database.

Karl, Z. (1996) "Divorce's toll on Children." *The American Enterprise*, v7, p.39(6). Retrieved November 15, 2009, from ProQuest database.

Lattimore, R. (2005) "Harnessing and Channeling African American Children's Energy in the Mathematics Classroom." *Journal of Black Studies*, 35:267. Retrieved November 3, 2009 from Proquest database.

Peterson, R.T. (2002) "The Depiction of African American Children's Activities in Television Commercials: An Assessment." *Journal of Business Ethics*, 36: 303–313. Retrieved October 12, 2002. From ProQuest database.

Supiano, B. (2009) "The Psychology of College Pricing." *The Chronicle of Higher Education*, 55: A.4 Retrieved April 24, 2009, from ProQuest database.

Tatum, A.W. (2000) "Breaking Down Barriers That Disenfranchise African American Adolescent Readers in Low-Level Tracks." *Journal of Adolescent & Adult Literacy*, 44: 52–64. Retrieved October 12, 2002, from ProQuest database.

Tatum, A.W. (2003) "All 'Degreed' Up and Nowhere to Go: Black Males and Literacy Education." *Journal of Adolescent & Adult Literacy*, 46: 620–623. Retrieved June 13, 2003, from ProQuest datatbase.

Wooster, M.M. (2000) "The Virtues of Learning at Home." *The American Enterprise*, 11: 56. Retrieved June 16, 2000, from Infotrac database.

Newspaper Articles

Pearl, L. (2003, October 1) "Homework Ranks Behind Other Pursuits." *Muskogee Daily Phoenix*, p. 1

Elrich, M. (1994, February 13) " The Stereotype Within; Why Students Don't Buy Black History Month." *The Washington Post*. pg. c.01

Peabody, Z. (2003, April 23) "Black Mayors Pessimistic about Federal Schools Act." *Houston Chronicle*, p. A29.

Hutchinson, E.O. (2002, December 17) "Exposing the Lie of Black Incompetence." *The Final Call*, p. 25.

United Nations Children's Fund (2003, September 9) "U.S. Education System Ranks Poorly among Developed Nations." *The Final Call*, p. 2.

Goleman, D. (1992, April 21) "Black Scientists Study the Pose of the Inner City." *The New York Times,* p.C7.

LeWine, H. (2008) "Lifestyle Changes May Reduce Risk of Prostate Cancer." *South Florida Sun-Sentinel*, p.16.

McManis, S. (2003, June 8) "Walking Children through Divorce: Kids' Turn Helps Parents Respond to the Needs of Sons and Daughters during a Family Split." *San Francisco Chronicle*, p. E1.

Reid, S.A. (2003, January 16) "Home School Advantage: African American Parents Look for Options Outside Public Education." *The Atlanta Journal-Constitution*, p.B1.

Jonsson, P. (2003, April 29) "Black Families Opt for Home Schooling.' *Seattle Times*, p. A5.

Squires, S. (2001, February 27). Soft Drinks, Hard Facts; The soda industry pays schools millions in its efforts to sell to students. But research suggests kids who drink a lot of soft drinks risk becoming fat, weak-boned, cavity- prone and caffeine-addicted. Sally Squires weighs the evidence. *The Washington Post*, p.T10.

Wells, V. (2009, May 11). "Extras round out high school life: Activities can develop skills, bring acceptance." *McClatchy-Tribune Business News.*

Music Albums

KRS ONE, "The Sneak Attack." (2001) A Koch Entertainment
    Company.

India Arie, "I'm Not My Hair." (2005) Motown Records